DR. PEACOCK AND HIS QUEST TO KNOW GOD

Gustav Shakefoot

Order this book online at www.trafford.com
or email orders@trafford.com

Most Trafford titles are also available at major online book retailers.

Printed in the United States of America.

ISBN: 978-1-4269-4261-7 (sc)
ISBN: 978-1-4269-4262-4 (hc)
ISBN: 978-1-4269-4263-1 (e)

Library of Congress Control Number: 2010913338

*Our mission is to efficiently provide the world's finest, most comprehensive book publishing
service, enabling every author to experience success. To find out how to publish your book,
your way, and have it available worldwide, visit us online at www.trafford.com*

Trafford rev. 09/07/2010

 www.trafford.com

North America & international
toll-free: 1 888 232 4444 (USA & Canada)
phone: 250 383 6864 ♦ fax: 812 355 4082

Table of Contents

Foreword

Are you frustrated? Where did you go wrong? Where did we go wrong?

"I tell you the truth, anyone who has faith in me will do what I have been doing. He will do even greater things than these, because I am going to the Father. And I will do whatever you ask in my name, so that the Son may bring glory to the Father. You may ask me for anything in my name and I will do it." (John 14:12-14 NIV).

These words of Jesus are promises. They tell us that anyone, not just some, a few or some super evangelist or preacher, will do what Jesus did. Not only what Jesus did but will do even greater things. What did Jesus do? He raised dead people, He healed all at many occasions, He cast out demons and evil spirits and preached the Good News to all. We have a great advantage over Jesus. He operated as the Son of Man and not as the Son of God. He operated under the Old Covenant. We operate under the New Covenant. He operated under Law we operate under Grace. He, Jesus, will do whatever we ask in His name and anything we ask in His name He will do. Why are we not seeing the results?

Let us not try to argue the 'problem' away but we must look at the problem bull's eye to find the answer.

In the Beginning.....

With chilling persistence the sirens howled to make everybody aware of the impending war. We wrote August 31. 1939. It was history in the making. That moment in time plunged the world into a crisis for five years, almost exactly by the day. World War Two in all its horrors, as predicted by the Virgin Mother of Jesus at Fatima, was upon us.

Tucked under the blankets in a hospital bed, a young mother in labor gave birth at that very instant to a baby boy. For more than a week she had been trying to give birth to her little boy but in vain. Only by the howling sirens, fear and anguish, brought about the last push. Times were harsh and unforgiving. Money was scarce. To pay for the hospital stay and medical attention she had to sacrifice inherited gold coins, coins she never intended to depart from. Days later she returned to her home where two siblings, a brother and a sister, were eagerly awaiting the new addition to the family. Life started in earnest. Within nine months the German Army invaded the Country. Endless marching soldiers resonated for days and weeks on end. Some of them, about one hundred and twenty to be more exact, sought forced shelter in their home. Customarily the soldiers overnighted in barns and haylofts. At times even that proved insufficient. In one particular barn one of the soldiers had to sleep with the male goat. Because of the very strong odor the male goat emanated, they would take turns every two hours. When Hans did not return past three hours, his soldiers' friends went and checked him out. To their surprise they found Hans fast asleep but the billy goat had taken off. (During war, showers and baths are off limit for most of the time).

The house of the little boy had three partitions. In the basement were the cows, the pigs, the chicken and the rabbits. The main floor housed the family of five and the top floor, the hayloft was taken over by the Germans. To grow up sandwiched between animals was no easy task for the little boy. The constant slamming of doors gave no peace to him. So he took his revenge by crying his lungs out, at night in particular. The soldiers hated him. They dubbed him, "the little stinker". The little stinker did his utmost best to live up to that name. Nevertheless he was favored by God and men. Men being his mother and father who took great pride to raise him as a Catholic Christian. Catholic stands for true. Recently many Christian denominations realized that for centuries they proclaimed the Roman Catholic Church as the true Church without knowing it. Nowadays they refer to the Catholic Church as the Roman Church. Does it matter to be born into any Christian denomination? Yes it does. Only those which are true offshoots of the Catholic Church are true Christians and not a sect or cult. Jesus instituted one Church and one Church only. He also acknowledged legitimate offshoots. Offshoots that have God the Father, God the Son and God the Holy Spirit as their God and who abide by Jesus Christ's teaching and doctrine. That doctrine is made tangible in the Word of God. It is the Bible. The New Testament was written under the guidance of the Holy Spirit by Matthew, Mark, Luke, John, Paul, Peter, James and Jude. All of them first hand Roman Catholics. Anyone who follows the teaching of the New Testament is by that very fact an offshoot of the Roman Catholic Church. A truth, hard to swallow by some. Some go even so far as to misinterpret and change the words of the Bible so that they differ from the Catholic Church. Others omit fifteen books of the Bible.

Books of the Bible

The Bible is divided into two chief parts: the 46 books of the Old Testament and the 27 books of the New Testament. The Old Testament was written over a period of about a thousand years and the New Testament over a period of one hundred years. The meaning of the word testament from both the Hebrew and the Greek languages is treaty or covenant. Covenant best captures the meaning of testament—Old Covenant and New Covenant.

Catholic and Protestant Bibles differ in that the Catholic Bibles contain the following fifteen extra books that the Protestant Bibles do not have:

1. First Esdras
2. Second Esdras

3. Tobit
4. Judith
5. The Additions to Esther
6. The Wisdom of Solomon
7. Ecclesiasticus, or the Wisdom of Jesus, the Son of Sirach
8. Baruch
9. The Letter of Jeremiah
10. The Prayer of Azariah and the Song of the Three Young Men
11. Susanna
12. Bel and the Dragon
13. The Prayer of Manasseh
14. First Maccabees
15. Second Maccabees

Since the little boy was born into a Catholic family, seven days later he was to be baptized. At baptism he became born of God. Born of his parents a sinner and born of God a righteous boy. He was a member of his human family and now he was also a member of God's family: God's Kingdom. As if he knew that the kingdom of God is voice activated he greatly exercised his voice apparatus to the detriment of all around him. Multiple births have a great advantage. When one cries loud enough, you will not hear the others.

Why Christian in the First Place?

There are many belief systems and surely one can find one that suits one's taste. Then why bother with Christianity? The answer lies in our human nature. Every human being needs to be a Christian. It is a matter of life and death. So why choose Christianity in the first place? Because there is no other faith or religion that can give any human being life of the spirit, mind and body and make us immortal and eternal according to God. "...that everyone who believes in him **may have eternal life**" (John 3:15 NIV).

"I give them eternal life, and they shall never perish; no one can snatch them out of my hand" (John 10:28 NIV). "For the wages of sin is death, but the gift of God is eternal life in Christ Jesus our Lord" (Romans 6:23 NIV).

"And this is the testimony: God has given us eternal life, and this life is in his Son. He who has the Son has life; he who does not have the Son of God does not have life" (1 John 5:11–12 NIV).

There is no other faith or religion that can give birth to any human being **to become a child, a son or a daughter, of God Almighty.** "How great is the love the Father has lavished on us, that we should be called children of God! And that is what we are!" (1 John 3:1–2 NIV).

"I will be a Father to you, and you will be my sons and daughters, says the Lord Almighty" (2 Corinthians 6:18 NIV).

There is no other faith or religion that **makes any human being a brother and a joint heir with Jesus Christ**. "Now if we are children, then we are heirs—heirs of God and co-heirs with Christ, if indeed we share in his sufferings in order that we may also share in his glory" (Romans 8:17 NIV).

There is no other faith or religion that can give any human being **spiritual power**. Spiritual power is released in our lives, able to transform us and those around us.

- The power of God's forgiveness that sets us free.
- The power that enables us to forgive those who have hurt us.
- The power to resist what we know is wrong.
- The power of God's love, which fills us with love for Him and for others.
- The power of God's Spirit, which brings us the new life of Jesus.
- The power to get wealth to be able to help others and to implement the kingdom of God here on earth. "His divine power has given us everything we need for life" (2 Peter1:3 NIV).

The restoration, the salvation, that new life of Jesus is free. You do not have to earn it, but you must ask for it; it does not come to you automatically. God respects your free will, even if it means that you may be lost forever. Four action words describe the course you must take to become born of God, to become a child of God:

Ask

You must ask Jesus to come into your heart. (Not your physical heart but the heart of your spirit) You invite Him into your dwelling.

Change Course

You ask for forgiveness for all that is wrong in your life, to save you and to set you free. And you determine to change course, to change position, to turn away from a sin position. Sin is a willful transgression of a natural or spiritual law. Those laws never change.

Believe

You believe in your heart that Jesus Christ is the Son of the Living God. You accept Him and He will accept you. Faith is the operating mode of your spirit.

Confess

You confess with your mouth that Jesus Christ is your Lord, Redeemer and Savior. Words, spoken words are powerful. The whole universe, including humankind, was created by spoken words not thoughts.

Here is a simple declaration that can bring you from darkness to light, from death to life, from bondage to freedom. It is the most important and the most powerful thing you can ever do for yourself; no one else can do it for you. Catholics call it life-giving prayer and the Protestants call it the sinner's prayer.

> Jesus, come into my heart and I will live for you. I ask you to forgive me, to save me and to set me free. I believe in my heart that you are the Son of the Living God and I declare that you are my Savior and Lord.

To believe and to profess your faith in Jesus Christ is but the first step to become born of God. As Mark 16:16 proclaims, "Whoever believes and is baptized will be saved" (NIV). So, baptism is the other step. Here Catholics and many Protestants differ greatly. For Catholics, you must be baptized; it is a sacrament. For Protestants, it is regarded as an ordinance and regarded as optional. Catholics profess and are baptized at the same time, as for the Protestants, depending on their affiliation, baptism may come anytime, weeks, months, years later or not at all.

Baptism

Baptism is absolutely necessary. Jesus Himself affirmed it in John 3:5, "In all truth I tell you, no one can enter the kingdom of God without being born through water and the Spirit" (NJB) and in John 3:22 we read, "Jesus went with his disciples into the Judean countryside and stayed there with them there and baptized" (NJB).

In Acts, the apostles did the same. "They accepted what he [the apostle Peter] said and were baptized! That very day about three thousand were added to their number" (Acts 2:41 NJB). The Protestant Martin Luther himself was convinced of the necessity of baptism. He wrote:

> Baptism is no human plaything but is instituted by God Himself. Moreover, it is solemnly and strictly commanded and we must be baptized or we shall not be saved. We are not to regard it as an indifferent matter, then, like putting on a new red coat. It is of the greatest importance that we regard baptism as excellent, glorious, and exalted" (Large Catechism 4:6, found in *Triglot Concordia: The Symbolical Books of the Ev. Lutheran Church*).

As a Christian it is hard to believe that many profess Jesus Christ but are not baptized even though the effects of baptism are so tremendous.

The Effects of Baptism

The baptismal effects are manifold. Those outstanding effects of water baptism should convince even the most reluctant person of its necessity.

Forgiveness of Sins

"'You must repent,' Peter answered, 'and every one of you must be baptized in the name of Jesus Christ **for the forgiveness of your sins, and you will receive the gift of the Holy Spirit'**" (Acts 2:38 NJB). All the sins a person ever committed will be forgiven and remembered no more. Once that happens, the baptized person receives the gift of the Holy Spirit. He, the Holy Spirit will dwell in him.

"It is the baptism corresponding to this water which saves you now—not the washing off of physical dirt but **the pledge of a good conscience** given to God through the resurrection of Jesus Christ" (1 Peter 3:21 NJB).

The Conscience

The conscience is an important part of everybody's spirit. It is the faculty that lets you distinguish between good and evil. It is humankind's inborn consciousness of a sense of right and wrong. It is a guiding recognition of right and wrong pertaining to your actions and the motives of your actions. It is your conscience that decides upon the moral standard of your actions and of your motives. It is that inner awareness of conforming to God's will or departing from it, resulting in a sense of approval or condemnation.

When your spirit is not born of God—dead in God's eyes—your conscience is not alive either. Nevertheless, your conscience is such a marvelous faculty created by God that even then you are able to recognize God. Romans 1:20 states, "For since the creation of the world God's invisible qualities—his eternal power and divine nature—have been clearly seen, being understood from what has been made, so that men are without excuse" (NIV) The human conscience bears witness to the existence of God.

A process of growth for maturity is required, which will not end until our spirit joins God in heaven. That growth can either be hastened or hampered depending upon us and the influences we allow to act upon our conscience.

You have enemies: yourself, the world and evil spirits. The world in this context means untruthfulness originating from persons other than you or from yourself. Evil spirits are Satan, demons and fallen angels.

You have friends: yourself, other persons, the Holy Spirit and good spirits (angels).

Friends, in this context means truthfulness originating from persons other than you, from yourself or from good spirits.

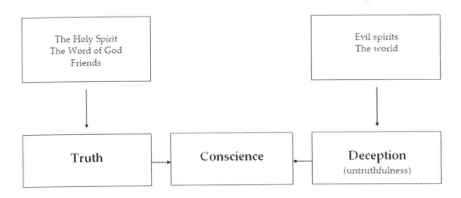

You yourself may influence your conscience in a good way or in a bad way. We train our conscience by the constant use of the Word of God. "But solid food is for the mature, who by constant use have trained themselves to distinguish good from evil" (Hebrews 5:14 NIV). Under wrong influences the conscience becomes defiled, polluted and evil. Such a conscience has been seared as with a hot iron, deceived to a high degree, unable to separate right from wrong.

By the new birth, being born of God, your conscience becomes alive. You yourself were unable to clear your conscience, but now the blood of Jesus Christ will accomplish exactly that, cleansing your conscience from acts that lead to death. The result is a pure, good and perfect conscience, void of any offence. "How much more, then, will the blood of Jesus Christ, who through the eternal Spirit offered himself unblemished to God, cleanse our consciences from acts that lead to death, so that we may serve the living God!" (Hebrews 9:14 NIV). Your conscience no longer condemns you and no longer downgrades your self-esteem. Some people are so bothered by their conscience for the things that they have done that it leads them to complete destruction by suicide.

Your conscience bears witness and testifies of good and evil. When there is something in your life that has to be changed, the Holy Spirit convicts you through your conscience. As a believer, your position has changed from condemnation, which leads to hopelessness and destruction, to conviction, which leads to hope and life.

In the final analysis, it is your heart that decides what action you take. Your heart may listen and follow the prompting of your conscience, or it may override it and follow its own desires. A good and perfect conscience is a safeguard that your heart should consult and ultimately abide by its counsel.

A New Creation

"So for anyone **who is in Christ, there is a new creation**: the old order is gone and a new being is there to see" (2 Corinthians 5:17 NJB).

> You cannot have forgotten that all of us, when **we were baptized into Christ Jesus**, were baptized into his death. So by our baptism into his death we were buried with him, so that as Christ was raised from the dead by the Father's glorious power, we too should begin living a new life (Romans 6:3–4 NJB).

"It is not being circumcised or uncircumcised that matters; but what matters **is a new creation**" (Galatians 6:15 NJB). The baptized person is baptized into Christ Jesus; he is in Christ. Therefore, he is a new creation and can start living a new life.

Circumcision of the Heart

"...and **real circumcision is in the heart,** a thing not of the letter but of the spirit" (Romans 2:29 NJB).

> In him you have been circumcised, with a circumcision performed, not by human hand, but **by the complete stripping of your natural self. This is circumcision according to Christ.** You have been buried with him by your baptism; by which, too, you have been raised up with him through your belief in the power of God who raised him from the dead (Colossians 2:11-12 NJB).

The circumcision of the heart performs a complete stripping of your natural self. Therefore it makes your spiritual birth complete—spirit, mind and body.

At baptism we are baptized with water, symbolizing our dying with Christ and our rising with Christ to the newness of life. We receive forgiveness of our sins, the circumcision of the heart, the indwelling of the Holy Spirit, the pledge of a good conscience, and we are baptized into Christ. The end result is a totally new creation.

One must realize that the necessity of water baptism is a normative rather than an absolute necessity. There are exceptions to water baptism. It is possible to be redeemed through 'baptism of blood' martyrdom for Christ. Or through 'baptism of desire' that is a conscious or even an unconscious desire for baptism. Jesus said, "I have a baptism to be baptized with" (Luke 12:50 KJ, as cited in Strong, 1989), when He had already been baptized.

He had come through water and blood, as John wrote, so that he might be baptized with water and glorified with blood. "He it is who came by water and blood, Jesus Christ, not with water alone but with water and blood, and it is the Spirit that bears witness, for the Spirit is Truth" (1 John 5:6.NJB).

"I have come to bring fire to the earth, and how I wish it were blazing already! There is a baptism I must still receive, and what constraint I am under until it is completed!" (Luke 12:49–50 NJB).

Those who, without knowing of Christianity but act under the inspiration of the Holy Spirit, seek God sincerely and strive to fulfill His will are saved even if they have not been baptized. "For since the creation of the world God's invisible qualities—his eternal power and divine nature—have been clearly seen, being understood from what has been made, so that men are without excuse" (Romans 1:20 NIV).

> But the other spoke up and rebuked him. "Have you no fear of God at all?" he said. "You got the same sentence as he did, but in our case we deserved it: we are paying for what we did. But this man has done nothing wrong." Then he said, "Jesus, remember me when you come into your kingdom."
>
> He answered him, "In truth I tell you, today you will be with me in paradise" (Luke 23:40–43 NJB).

Infant Baptism

Infant baptism stands out as a bone of contention among many Protestants. Some claim that infants are incapable of being baptized validly because infants, they say, are unable to be born again due to their physical immaturity and having not yet reached the age of reason. They claim infants and young children are born again automatically but must accept Jesus Christ when they reach the age of reason in order to reach heaven. What does the Bible say about it? "The promise is for you and your children and for all who are far off—for all whom the Lord our God will call" (Acts 2:39 NIV). This command is universal, not restricted to adults only. The term children includes infants. If we prevent infants from being baptized, we are making a statement that they are unable to have spiritual life, which is nonsense. Jesus set a precedent, as found in Luke 18:15–17:

> People even brought babies to him, for him to touch them; but when the disciples saw this they scolded them. But Jesus called the children to him and said, "Let the little children come to me, and do not stop them; for it is to such as these that the kingdom of God belongs. In truth I tell you, anyone who does not welcome the kingdom of God like a little child will never enter it" (NJB).

Those opposing infant baptism, on grounds that infants are incapable of having faith and since faith is required to be baptized, should carefully consider the following. The Lord did not require infants or young children to make a conscious decision for him; the Godparents or the parents stand for them. As the faith of others can heal a person, so the faith of others can bring life in baptism for their child. The cure of the paralytic man in Luke 5:17–26 shows us how the faith of others was instrumental in getting the man healed.

"After she [Lydia] and her household had been baptized she kept urging us" (Acts 16:15 NJB).

"Late as it was, he took them to wash their wounds, and was baptized then and there with all his household." (Acts 16:33 NJB).

"Yes, I did baptize the family of Stephanas, too" (1 Corinthians 1:16 NJB). There must have been babies in those families, at least in some of them if not in all of them. The Catholic Church always taught infant baptism and baptized babies. It follows apostolic tradition, tradition of the apostles inspired by the Holy Spirit. Apostolic tradition has nothing in common with human tradition that makes the Word of God ineffective. The Early Church did not have the New Testament so they had to rely on apostolic tradition.

Baptism is the circumcision of the heart. In fact baptism has replaced circumcision of the flesh. It too required faith for the adults but not for infants of believers. "In him you have been circumcised, with a circumcision performed, not by human hand, but by the complete stripping of your natural self. This is circumcision according to Christ" (Colossians 2:11 NJB). In Old Testament times, if a man wanted to become a Jew, he had to believe in the God of Israel and be circumcised. In the New Testament, if one wants to become a Christian, one must believe in God and Jesus and be baptized. In the Old Testament, those born of Jewish households could be circumcised in anticipation of the Jewish faith in which they would be raised. Thus, in the New Testament, those born in Christian households can be baptized in anticipation of the Christian faith in which they will be raised.

Many Protestants who object to infant baptism dedicate their children to God as a substitute to baptism.

The Catholic Church recognizes as valid baptism a baptism by immersion, lowering of the body into the water; by aspersion, the sprinkling of the body with water; and by infusion, the pouring of water over the body. Catholics also recognize as valid baptisms performed by non-Catholics. Anyone may baptize an infant in danger of death; even an aborted fetus should be baptized. If no sign of life is present, then the fetus should be baptized conditionally. Baptism is conferred conditionally when there is doubt concerning a previous baptism or the disposition of the person to be baptized. Through baptism one becomes a member of the body of Christ.

Adult Baptism

Anabaptists, such as the Baptists, the Mennonites, the Hutterites etc., do not recognize infant baptism. That doctrine stems from a violent past. Luther, Calvin and Zwingli considered the position of the Anabaptists heresy. Their main tenet was that baptism is for adults only, making infant baptism invalid. The term 'Anabaptist' (re-baptizer) was pinned on them by their adversaries. It all started in the sixteenth century. In Zurich's City State, as in the rest of the Christian World, every newborn child was baptized. City Council decreed (January 17, 1525) to have all babies baptized within eight days of birth, or the parents would face banishment from the territory. The Anabaptists would not baptize the babies and would re-baptize the adults who were already baptized as babies. On March 17, 1526, the Zurich Council lost patience and decided if they found anyone re-baptizing they would be put to death by drowning. Their reasoning was if the heretics want water let them have it. So, many fled to Germany and Austria. It was like jumping from the frying pan into the fire. In 1529, the Imperial Diet of Spyer proclaimed Anabaptism a heresy, and every court in Christendom was obliged to condemn the heretics to death. Luther joined forces with the Catholics, and they persecuted the Anabaptists intensely. Among the early Anabaptist's missionaries to Tyrol was George Blaurock, a former Catholic priest. He was burned at the stake on September 6, 1529. So was Michael Sattler, a former Benedictine monk, burnt at the stake in Rottenburg-am-Neckar in 1527. Many thousand Anabaptists were executed during the Reformation by fire, by sword but mostly by water. Society is a lot more tolerant nowadays, and Anabaptism is still very much practiced in Protestant circles.

Salvation Explained

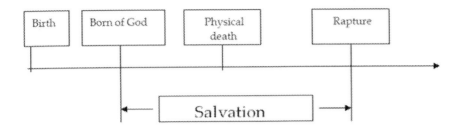

Salvation starts when a person is born of God and stretches up to and including the Rapture. At the Rapture the redemption of the believer is accomplished and finished for all those who died a physical death before the Rapture took place and for all those who will be alive when the Rapture occurs.

"Whoever believes and is baptized will be saved, whoever does not believe will be condemned."(Mark 16:16 NJB). The key is to believe, baptism becomes irrelevant if the person to be baptized does not believe. Take any person and baptize that person and baptism is totally useless. Take a person who believes and baptize that person, now that person is born of God and all the effects of baptism are active in that person. Being born of God comprises two steps: believing and being baptized. Too many only take the first step. Their argument is that the thief on the cross was not baptized either. "Then he said, "Jesus remember me when you come into your kingdom." Jesus answered him, "I tell you the truth, today you will be with me in paradise." (Luke 23:42-43 NIV).

The thief could have desired baptism or received the baptism of blood. Who are we to judge God's wisdom! How important is baptism to God? The last command Jesus gave His disciples before taken up to heaven is this, "Therefore go and make disciples of all nations, baptizing them in the name of the Father and of the Son and of the Holy Spirit." (Matthew 28:19 NIV). The effects of baptism are manifold. Obviously these effects do not take place in a person who is not baptized. Believing is your initiative, the effects of baptism are God's response to you.

Some Protestants make it a life duty to get the Catholics 'saved'. It's like selling ice to an Eskimo or sand to an Arab. Their argument is that the Catholics never said the 'sinner's prayer'. It should be the other way around because many Protestants are not baptized. The 'believing part' should not be separated from baptism. The Catholic Church does not separate step one: believing and step two baptizing. The priest or any other person depending on the circumstances ask the person to be baptized specific questions: renouncing Satan and his work, believing in Jesus Christ as Saviour and redeemer as well as in the basic doctrine outlined in the Creed. If the answer is yes only then is that person baptized. To be born of God comprises two steps but one action.

For infants the sponsors stand in for the believing part. The baptized baby is born of God with all the benefits of baptism in effect. When the infants reach the age of reason they will proclaim the 'life giving prayer' before receiving their first communion, sealing with their own will what the sponsors did for them as infants.

At the Reformation 'works' became a dirty word. Many Protestant writers claim that Mother Teresa is doomed because of her good works. I myself was the victim of a so called 'works' zealot. Once that man lay hold on a book about Mother Teresa, he pulled the book from my shelf and ripped the pages out while screaming loudly, "She is damned." The next verse of the Bible is for everyone but especially for the 'works' zealots. "Anyone, then, who knows the good he ought to do [good works] and doesn't do it, sins." (James 4:17 NIV). Martin Luther thought works of flesh would get him saved. Then he read Romans 3:28 and realized that he was wrong. James 2:24 declares the contrary. Luther promised his PhD. to anyone who could harmonize both references. It became his nightmare and he even tried to get James totally removed from the Bible. "For we maintain that a man is justified [saved] by faith apart from observing the law [works]." (Romans 3:28 NIV). The law refers to rules and regulations and not works of love. "You see that a person is justified [saved] by what he does and not by faith alone."(James 2:24 NIV). Romans refers to be born of God and James refers to 'work out your salvation' during your life span. There is no contradiction whatsoever, it is just common sense. Luther regarded baptism as absolutely necessary for being born of God but many contemporary Protestants do not.

They regard 'baptism' as 'works'. Clinton E. Arnold chairman of the Department for the New Testament at Talbot School of Theology states, (on page 20 Concerning Baptism Discipleship Journal Jan/Feb 2006 Issue 151) "Neither circumcision nor baptism -both being "works"- can bestow salvation".

How can baptism be 'works'? Baptism is an outward sign established by Jesus Christ to confer inward grace by the power of the Holy Spirit.

People who believe that baptism is 'works' do not understand how God works among His people.

Another wide spread heresy claims that salvation (being born of God) cannot be lost.

The call of a Christian is not a call of passivity, a call to wait and see, a call to lay back, but a call to go forward, to evangelize your surrounding, a call of constant, fervent zeal in fulfilling God's will in your life, a call to bring about God's kingdom on earth. We are created in Christ Jesus to do good works.

"...but anyone who stands firm to the end will be saved" (Matthew 24:13 NJB). Everybody has talents, natural and spiritual talents. Those talents ought to be used to bring about God's kingdom here on earth. We will be judged according to what we did with our talents. We read in the Bible, in the parable of the talents, that the one who received one talent buried it and did nothing with it. It was taken from him. "And throw that worthless servant outside, into the darkness, where there will be weeping and gnashing of teeth!" (Matthew 25:30 NIV). It is a picture of eternal damnation. It does not sound like salvation.

"Remember God's severity as well as his goodness: his severity to those who fell, and his goodness to you as long as you persevere in it; if not, you too will be cut off." (Romans 11:22 NJB). Persevere in God's goodness, as you love Him and your fellow men.

> "...and you may be sure that anyone who tramples on the Son of God, and who treats *the blood of the covenant* which sanctified him as if it were not holy, and who insults the Spirit of grace, will be condemned to a far severer punishment." (Hebrews 10:29 NJB).

"Do not be afraid of those who kill the body but cannot kill the soul; fear him rather who can destroy both body and soul in hell" (Matthew 10:28–29 NJB). Soul stands for your spiritual, your supernatural nature. Salvation can be lost by the choices you make, by your reaction to influence.

"..and anyone who has escaped the pollution of the world by coming to know our Lord and Savior Jesus Christ, and who then allows himself to be entangled and mastered by it a second time, ends up by being worse than he was before" (2 Peter 2:20 NJB).

> "How much more can we be sure, therefore, that, now we have been justified by his death, we shall be saved through him from

the retribution of God. For if, while we were enemies, we were reconciled to God through the death of his Son, how much more can we, be sure that, being now reconciled, we shall be saved by his life." (Romans 5:9–10 NJB).

Many will say to me on that day, "Lord, Lord, did we not prophesy in your name, and in your name drive out demons and perform many miracles?" Then I will tell them plainly, "I never knew you. Away from me, you evildoers!" (Matthew 7:22–23 NIV).

"I know your deeds, that you are neither cold nor hot. I wish you were either one or the other! So, because you are lukewarm—neither hot nor cold—I am about to spit you out of my mouth." (Revelation 3:15–16 NIV).

How you live and end your earthly life, the choices you made, the work you did or did not do, all determine your final salvation.

"To God we are the fragrance of Christ, both among those who are being saved and among those who are on the way to destruction; for these last, the smell of death leading to death, but for the first, the smell of life leading to life." (2 Corinthians 2:15–16 NIV).

God uses different criteria to deal with unbelievers, sinners, immature believers or mature believers. To whom much is giving much is required.

The verse 24 of James chapter 2 (NIV), "You see that a person is justified [saved] by what he does and not by faith alone" applies to the time span from being born of God to the physical death of that person. That time span is the 'work phase'. Many believers are taught to believe that being born of God is salvation accomplished. They do not need the five fold ministry to bring them to maturity. They only need the evangelist and the 'assassin' to catapult them into heaven (quote from Charlie at a conference in September 2006 in Abbotsford Canada).

The work phase is divided into two sub-phases: the love your God phase and the love others phase. The work phase is characterized by love. "The only thing that counts is faith expressing itself through love." (Galatians 5:6 NIV). This is the time to do good works as mentioned in verse 10 chapter 2 of Ephesians (NIV), "For we are God's workmanship created in Christ Jesus to do good works, which God prepared in advance for us to do." It is the time to work out our salvation. "Continue to work out your salvation with fear and trembling, for it is God who works in you to will and to act according to his good pleasure."(Philippians 2:12-13 NIV). For God to work in you and through you, you must abide in Him.

"Remain in me, and I will remain in you. No branch can bear fruit by itself; it must remain in the vine. Neither can you bear fruit unless you remain in me.

I am the vine; you are the branches. If a man remains in me and I in him, he will bear much fruit; apart from me you can do nothing. If anyone does not remain in me, he is like a branch that is thrown away and withers; such branches are picked up, thrown into the fire and burned. If you remain in me and my words remain in you, ask whatever you wish, and it will be given you. This is my Father's glory, that you bear much fruit, showing yourselves to be my disciples." (John 15:4-8 NIV). It is clear that without Jesus we can do nothing. Therefore for the work phase to be effective on must rely on the grace of God at all times.

(reprinted from "Who is Your Father?")

War Years

Once the Country Luxembourg was invaded and occupied by the German Army, an oppressive Germanisation took place. The Nazis regarded the Luxemburgers a Germanic ethnic group. Therefore a formal annexation to Germany was not necessary. French as a second language was outlawed. French names of people, streets and towns were given Germanic names. Teachers, officials and any influential people had to join Nazi organizations. They were forced to collaborate with Germany. Those who refused were tortured and sent to the notorious concentration camps. Many did perish. After the war about two thousand collaborators were found guilty of treason, some were executed others remained jailed until the 1950s when most of them were amnestied. All the while the Nazis kept a central data base of almost everybody's opinion of the Reich. Even the clothing was censored. One was not allowed to wear a beret. It was deemed to be too French. All by-laws were strictly enforced. A pooping man was caught in the public park. The officer demanded his papers. The man handed over his toilet papers thinking the officer had to poop too. But the officer wanted his identification papers. They made an example out of the pooping man.

Every male born between 1920 and 1929 was drafted into the German Wehrmacht. About forty percent refused. They either fled to Briton or hid within the Country's border. Each time the Gestapo caught a hiding youth, he and his family were deported to the concentration camps. That family was immediately replaced by a German family from South-Tyrol or East-Germany.

The little boy's uncle Peter hid two young men in his house. He was on the constant lookout for the Gestapo. He became neurotic that almost did his family in. One day the Gestapo came towards his house. Peter pulled a pistol and was ready to shoot the commander. The little boy's father wrestled him to the ground thus preventing a bloodbath. The commander and his soldiers wanted some information about rumors of an uprising against the Nazis. That uprising happened August 1942. It was quenched violently with thousands being tortured and many send to the death camps. Nevertheless that uprising of such a small Country against such a powerful oppressor became an inspiration to all occupied countries. Only two such public uprising took place during the war. From then on the resistance went totally underground.

Not only the young male had to serve in the German Army but the young adult girls were recruited against their will to serve in the Reichsarbeitsdient.

The best time to be is always home even in times of war. One third of the Luxemburger population fled ahead of the invading German Army. It did not help at all. The places they fled to were invaded too. The little boy's father had the insight to stay put and he continued to work in a steel assembly plant. One day while cycling home from work he was intercepted by the Gestapo. His crime was pedaling in the dark without head lights. He invented a new German name for himself. The Gestapo ordered him to present himself at the Villa Pauly the next day. He never went there. He knew that the Villa Pauly was the Gestapo's headquarter: a symbol of torture and terror. People who went in alive were carried out in body bags days later. The Villa Pauly lay peacefully admits neatly tended flower gardens and whispering water fountains. Appearance does not always portray reality. Occupying armies often rely on local food supplies. The Germans were not any different. The little boy's parents had to provide potatoes, eggs, milk and butter (they churned the milk to make the butter) for the hungry German bunch especially the officers. Cows do become pregnant from time to time and when they do the milk factory goes dry. Every farm boy knows this but not the German Zahlmeister (treasurer). He held the purse and the authority to inspect the food supply. The Zahlmeister did not believe the boy's father and insisted he would get milk from the pregnant cow. He took a stool and a milk pail ready to do his deed. By now, Mazette, the cow was startled, "No, you do not touch my nipples, they are already sore. Don't you dare touch my tits, you idiot." The moment the Zahlmeister touched and pulled the nipples, Mazette wagged him with her tail in the face. The hind leg did the rest. He found himself in the cow's manure. He never tried again. Mazette gave birth to twin calves. The identical twins turned out to be a real blessing. As long as the calves were kept in different locations nobody realized that there were two. The little boy ate some real veal at his tender age. The German officers devoured the other one. Things do not always are the way they seem to be. For example look at the next scene of a moving train in the hilly landscape of France during German occupation. In one compartment are sitting a mature German officer beside him a young girl and opposite of them an older lady and a young Frenchman. No one talks. All are quite busy thinking their own thoughts. The train snakes joyfully around a bend and enters the darkness of a tunnel. There are no lights on because of war time. All of a sudden a loud smack followed by a hefty slap is heard and before anyone could voice an opinion, daylight floods the compartment again. Everybody is on edge. The face of the German officer is red, dark red. Now everybody's thoughts are focused, focused on one thing only: the red cheek of the officer. What happened?

The German officer, "This young Frenchman kisses the girl and I get slapped for it." The old lady, "All respect for the young girl. She slapped the officer when he kissed her." The young girl, "I am outraged. I expected to be kissed and not the old lady." Here comes the truth. The Frenchman chuckles inside, "Well done pal." He kissed the back of his hand, slapped the officer and got away with it.

The Zahlmeister was a real pain in the behind. He constantly urged the little boy's father to sell him their home. Johann (the little boy's father) was wise to thwart every attempt with success. While the war and the German occupation were wearing on, the people tried to make the best of the situation. The sky was filled with airplanes. The constant droning of the airplane, day and night, became unnoticeable. People were so used to it that when it stopped for a short time, everybody thought something was wrong. It was like the throwing of the boots in this episode. A laborer who lived in an apartment complex came home late at night, every night. After about half an hour he was ready to retire. He would remove his heavy boots, throw them in one of the corners of the bedroom and go to sleep. All the apartment neighbors were very upset with the nightly ritual. This went on for quite some time. Finally someone mustered enough courage to tell him to cut the boot throwing out. At first he would not heed the demand. One day he had a change of heart. He went quietly to bed while all his neighbors were anxiously waiting for the throwing of the boots. So they too could go to sleep. They waited and waited. In their desperation they went to his door and shouted, "For heaven's sake throw your boots."

The flying wounded bombers relieved themselves from their deadly loads before crashing in the hope the crew may survive. After the war, hundred of unexploded bombs were found in the forests in the soft soil. The German soldiers moved on in September of 1944 with the Allied forces at their tail. Luxembourg was liberated but not for very long. The American soldiers moved in where the little boy lived. For the first time ever he tasted chocolate (was it ever good), oranges and grapefruit juice. He never lost the taste for chocolate. "Dead by chocolate" applies to him to this very day.

Next to the boy's home was a large estate, castle and all. The estate was made up of hundreds of hectares of forest, orchards, pastures and ponds filled with fish. The American Army took hold of the estate. It became the headquarter of their operations including antiaircraft batteries. What a great thing to be protected like that. On the other hand it also attracted the German retaliation like a magnet. The entrance to the estate was flanked by concrete walls and guarded twenty four hours daily by the military police. The little boy would visit the guards, he would bring them red wine his father had made. The red wine was the carrot to grease the guards' hands. It worked. They stuffed his pockets with chocolate and other goodies. In time the soldiers became fond of the little boy and played war games with him. They dressed him in an army jacket, put a helmet on his head and stuck him in a Sherman tank. They taught him how to stir the metal monster around the town square in the shape of a triangle.

By December of 1944 the German Army invaded Luxembourg a second time. This time they came to fight the Battle of the Bulge. The bulge does not mean the spare tire some people wear around their waist but the geographical location centered around the Ardennes in Northern Luxembourg. The Battle of the Bulge became the bloodiest battle U.S. forces had to fight in World War Two. It started December sixteen 1944 and concluded January twenty six 1945. About an equal amount of casualties and losses were reported on both sides. The difference was that the Allied Forces were the winners. (840 000 Allied soldiers versus 500 000 German soldiers, 80 000 to 95 000 killed, wounded or missing on either side.)

During these weeks of fierce fighting the sky was constantly lit, very noticeable at night. It could be seen hundreds of kilometers away. The Germans thought if they would win this battle they still could win the war. The little boy's uncle Jim lived in that area. He was caught by the Gestapo at his farm house. The uncle escaped from the German soldiers on Christmas day in 1944. It meant he had to run across fields into the darkness of a dense forest. He kept running when all of a sudden his departed mother appeared to him and commanded him not to go any further. Exhausted he dropped to the ground. When daylight broke, he realized the abyss just feet away from where he lay. Had he gone any further the night before, he would have fallen to his certain death. This was a direct intervention of a departed saint of the glorious church to help a member of the militant Church.

Just before Christmas 1944 the American antiaircraft battery shot down a German fighter airplane. Part of it fell only meters away from the little boy's home. The main body crashed in a nearby hotel, which burst into flames and totally destroyed it. The tables were set for a Christmas eve party for about one hundred twenty soldiers. Nobody was in the hotel at the time not even the owner, therefore nobody got hurt A real miracle you could say, but the little boy's uncle Peter saw it differently. "It was an act of God", he would say. The hotel owner, a lady, would use Peter's milk to wash and bath herself and buy milk from someone else for herself and her guests to drink. The milk went to his head, especially when he was drunk. He would cry like a baby. In the end it was not the milk that did him in but alcohol. On his dead bed the doctor prescribed him a bottle of the best wine and said, "Drink, drink it all. It will be your last." It was.

One of the most outstanding but controversial U.S. Army officer was General George Patton. He is well remembered for his "scientific" and colorful language. He did not get along with General Montgomery. Hitler called him, "That crazy cowboy general" and hoped he would be relieved of his duties and sent home. It almost happened. When the 101st Airborne division was encircled by the Germans in Bastogne, Patton moved his troupes within forty eight hours more than one hundred kilometers to liberate them. They ran out of food and ammunition and no help could come from the sky because of very bad weather. Patton needed twenty four hours of clear sky. He ordered the Third Army Chaplain James O'Neil to come up with a prayer so God would grant him the good weather request. The weather cleared soon after the prayer. Patton decorated the Chaplain with a Bronze Star on the spot. Never in history did any army engage so many enemy armies in such a short time. It was one of the worst winters recorded. No sleep for any soldier in those forty eight hours. They liberated Bastogne in time.

Patton was a real character. He only fired one general and only after repeated warnings whereas General Bradley relieved more than a dozen generals with little or no provocation. It was that same General Bradley who was detained at a checkpoint, suspected of being a German infiltrator. Some German soldiers dressed in Allied uniforms (speaking English very well) infiltrated the army ranks. To weed them out, checkpoints were established and every one had to answer skill testing questions. General Bradley was asked, "What is the capital of Illinois?" He answered correctly, "Springfield." The GI who questioned him thought the capital was "Chicago", hence the detention of Bradley. The German commanders hated Patton. They said, "If war does not kill him the lack of it will. It did. On December 9th 1945 Patton went pheasant hunting in the countryside of Mannheim. He took his chief of staff and a driver with him. Past a railway crossing they were hit by an army truck (American technical support). Patton was thrown forward (He was sitting in a back seat) hitting his head against the metal partition between back and front seats. Patton was paralyzed while his chief of staff and the driver were both alright. Patton died of embolism on December 21st 1945 with his wife at his side. He was buried at the Luxemburger Army cemetery in Hamm. On March 19. 1947 he was moved to the U.S.A. Britain, France, Belgium and Luxembourg highly decorated Patton for his outstanding achievements during World War Two.

Hunting can be quite dangerous, and lead poisoning often is the outcome. Dick Cheney, Vice President of the Bush Administration, went hunting with some of his friends. He shot only one not two. "It was an accident," he claimed. Fortunately the victim survived. Shortly after that incident, President Bush met with the Mexican President Vicente Fox. Rumor has it that Mr. Bush was not happy with the outcome, so he phoned his friend Mr. Tony Blair. Bush asked Blair to invite Mr. Fox to a fox hunt. He also urged him to invite Mr. Cheney as well. Mr. Fox gladly received the invitation, but when he realized that Mr. Cheney was invited too he quickly declined: better save than sorry or worse.

In March 1945 Luxembourg was liberated a second time, this time for good. In the Northern part of Luxembourg where the Battle of the Bulge was fought, hardly any house or structure was standing. The destruction was complete.

Luxembourg did not have an army before World War Two, due to a restriction imposed by the 1867 Treaty of London. After the War there were plenty of volunteer soldiers and they took their revenge on Germany. They occupied part of Saarburg (1948) and the area of Bitburg/Eiffel from which they withdrew in July 1955. Peace and prosperity followed 1945. Unexploded ammunition of all sorts were found by unsuspecting individuals. The little boy found a live hand grenade. He was so intrigued by the device, he had to get to the bottom (centre) of it. He took a hammer and hammered it so hard the lever broke off. The safety pin with the ring to pull grabbed his attention. At that very moment his mother saw him, she froze then yelled, "Get away from it, it is a hand grenade." The boy froze too. His father disposed of the grenade. That was a close call. It was the same spot years later lightning struck the boy on a Sunday afternoon. The lightning ripped a gapping hole in the neighbor's house (stone wall). God and His angels protected the rascal like so many times.

Children play with toys, hide and seek and doctor. The boy's neighbor had three daughters. The youngest was the same age as the little boy. They were very good friends and they liked to play doctor together. He showered her with many gifts his mother's best jewelry including her gold wrist watch. In turn his girlfriend let him undress her completely. He was totally fascinated (he still is today). Alas they were caught. He is grateful to his mother that she did not overreacted but seized the opportunity to give them the first formal sex education. She did not use medical terms, slang nor childish words to describe and explain the sex organs. For her a penis was a penis and a vulva a vulva. If, we as parents give our children the right information with the proper terms and are honest with them, then they will always come to us when they need advice. Sex education begins at day one and continues throughout all adult's life.

A six year old girl was ask on TV (children and God), "Does God make mistakes?" "Oh yes," she replied. "Can you give an example," the host asked. Her reply was quick, "Sex." May be she never played doctor. Here is what the late Pope John the 23rd had to say about women. "There are three things that can ruin a man: women, gambling and farming. My father chose the most boring one: farming." He was never late to tell a joke or a funny story.

It is time to name the little boy. At baptism he was given four names, one of which was the name of the pope of that time. Here we call him Peacock. It is his real nickname, given to him by his friends. "Be polite and accept the gift people give you," his mother told him often. He likes the name "Peacock" even though he got that name many years later. Burglars came to his house and took things that belonged to him and left. He was not going to let that happen again. He installed an alarm to scare any intruder off before they would break a door or window. The key was to set the alarm off as soon as anybody would step on the welcoming doormat. One big problem arose: he did not factor in the roaming around of his peacock. In no time the fowl figured it out. Whenever the alarm was set, the peacock would jump on the mat. You guessed it, it would set it off. The sound of the siren excited the peacock to a very high degree. He became addicted to it. Each time he would spread his plumage to its full extend and proudly strutting around as if he were in the presence of the peahen. The peacock had to go. He fetched hundred twenty dollars at a local auction. Days later Peacock's wife, Jennifer, stepped on the mat and she too set the siren off but Peacock could not........ When his friends heard the story they called him, "Dr. Peacock". For now we call him, "Peacock" and later when he is older "Dr. Peacock". He is a doctor in NO. You are more successful in life when you have a PhD of some sort.

School Years

The first day little Peacock went to school was a real shocker. It was not so much the day than the teacher: a plump middle-aged lady who reacted to the name of Ms. Apple. Her head was totally shaven. It seemed the hair went underground. Bushy hair sprouted under the nose, from the nose and ears as well. It was good that she wore a dress and not her prison garb. Just days ago she was released from jail for being a German collaborator. The lack of teachers got her off the hook before time fully served. A five pound bag filled with delicious candies adorned her desk. We boys and girls languished for those candies but most of them found their way to Ms. Apple's mouth. Was it the candies or boredom of the class that made Ms. Apple dose off several times a day, we do not know. During her napping times her pupils came alive. We read her like a book. Writing exams became a piece of cake, we just waited for her to fall asleep. The trick was to insert some mistakes, here and there. Some of the students were not very bright. One did first grade for the sixth time. Poor fellow, it was understandable, he went to school during war times. Some of the students wrote everything right except for the last paragraph. That was a big mistake. You need to be alert to cheat.

Politics were to blame for a classroom full of misfits. There were two classrooms both harbored boys and girls. The city council assigned the children of the less educated parents (mostly from poor families) to Ms. Apple (the jailbird) and the better off children to a young male teacher (with no underground hair growth). Another remarkable thing was that the village was the most notorious place for crime, bullying and rowdiness of the whole Country. Just mentioning the village name and anyone would keep their distance. Divorce was not tolerated at all. One man axed his wife. Another surprised his wife at Christmas Eve with a boyfriend in bed. She (naked) was frying eggs for the lover. The enraged husband grabbed her and literally fried her naked behind in the frying pan. She died from the burns. He got two years probation.

To keep us in line Ms. Apple would spank us with a wooden rod on the bare bum. The other teacher (the one without sprouting underground hair) would not do that but he would hammer our knuckles with a wooden square ruler. At times he would throw the ruler at us, so we learned quickly to duck. No one would complain, if our parents got to know the abuse, we were in for another spanking. They called it, "discipline". From time to time the whole class would make a field trip. Actually it was a forest trip with the purpose of cutting spanking rods. It was to our advantage to cut soft wood rods not oak. Our bums were very grateful for the consideration. Ms. Apple lived above the classroom. Many houses did not have their running water restored. The stronger boys had to fetch pails of water from a well and bring it to the teacher's apartment. A few pails went under her bed not by themselves but we poured it out under her bed. Shortly after that the classroom ceiling would start to leak, drip, drip, which turned into shouts of pain and fiery buttocks cheeks.

The classroom was heated by a gigantic wooden stove. From time to time wood blocs had to be added to keep the fire from dying out. It is remarkable how those with the least intelligence came up with the bright idea to insert some live ammunition (there was plenty of unexploded ammunition in the forests and fields) to the red hot coal. The consequence of the ensuing big bang catapulted most of us in a fast growing up mode, others still did not behave in grade six.

All the desks were outfitted with ink fountains. Ballpoint pens were not yet invented and ink pens were in vogue. We were wondering what would happen if yeast was added to the ink? It sounded like another bright idea. Yeast was plentiful in every kitchen. Most people would bake their own bread with yeast, how delicious! Before class we would pour yeast kernels in every ink pot except our own. That proved to be a big mistake that gave us away. It was the custom to pray before class. That day we prayed with intense fervency for a greater chemical reaction, and reaction we got. Ink was bubbling all over the desks, total chaos reigned with shouting and screaming. We did it, we triumphed but not for long. In those days things like that always found their way to our parents. That spelled double trouble. To our parents Christian education seemed to be the answer to curb our mischievous behavior.

Christian Education

Most of the Country's population was Catholic with just a handful of Protestants and some well accepted Jews. The Protestants were regarded as heretics but not so the Jews. Before the German occupation there were about three thousand eight hundred Jews in Luxembourg. When the Nurenberg Laws concerning the Jews were introduced by Gauleiter Simon, most of the Jews fled or went underground. By the end of 1941 all those who could be found were sent to the concentration camps (out of 683 only 43 survived). Simon declared Luxembourg by June 1943 a Jewish free state. Alfred Oppenheimer was one of the Jewish survivor. His wife was killed and his son was gassed. Oppenheimer was a member of the Jewish Council and a witness at the trial of Adolf Eichman. He returned to Luxembourg and lived to a ripe old age of ninety.

The relation between Church and State is unique in Luxembourg. The parish priest draws a salary (substantial) from the government. The dwelling is provided and so is the church building itself. The maintenance and upkeep is the responsibility of the municipality and so are the utilities bills. Once you are a parish priest you have it made (financially). The parish priest is responsible for the spiritual wellbeing of the parish including weekly Christian education classes from grade one to eight.

My village, with only a handful of households, had neither school nor church. Located on top of a mountain (small) we had to go down to the valley, the neighboring village, for school and church. Two villages but one municipality surrounded by fifteen square kilometers of mostly forests, some fields and some pastures. A perfect environment to grow up in. School kept us occupied six days a week with Tuesdays and Thursdays' afternoons free. Tracking to and from school and church (12 kilometers per day) kept us fit and ready to sleep anytime after 9 P.M.. The free afternoons we would roam the forests. Sometimes we would bring home a wild rabbit. I caught two with my bare hands. I was quick. One time I saw a wild rabbit in his den under dry branches. He had no chance to escape. Another time a rabbit was hiding under thick grass, thinking I could not see it. Deadly mistake, I grabbed it and turned its neck. Bringing home venison was fine but the wild instinct in us went further. The neighbor's estate had three large ponds teaming with fish. We never were taught fishing. By the way that's wasting time and boring. We simply drained one of the ponds of most of its water. The fish lay around just for the picking. We also encountered gaggles of geese. I run after one in particular, caught it and turned its neck. At that moment my conscience kicked in. This is not right, a Christian will not do such a thing. I buried the goose under a tree and we all went home, sad. My mother found out and told us to get the goose. After we ate the goose I felt better. A lot better in comparison to the time we ate in a Chinese restaurant. Half through our dinner the waiter asked, "Are you still feeling alright?" On purpose we did not touch one dish, we intended to take it home. A little time later the same waiter pointed at that dish, "I would not eat that dish either."

Every student was required to attend mass before starting school classes. During winter it meant to shuffle and tread through two to three feet of snow. Some of us boys helped the organist to ring the church bells and to activate air for the organ. The organ towered high on the balcony. We did also sing and misbehaved. The organist was the village butcher. During the week he did not change his butchering clothing, hence he smelled the pig, the cow and the occasional goat or horse. Sunday afternoon and evening he spent time with his drinking buddies in the local pub. Whenever an occasion presented itself he would treat a hobo with all the beer the fellow could drink with one condition: the hobo had to eat a whole Camembert cheese all by himself. That kind of cheese plus the beer proofed fatal for the hobo's pants. Once the fermentation took place there was no toilet close enough to receive the load.

During mass we boys tried the butcher-organist's patience. He did not say a word but grabbed a five pound hymn book and threw it at us. Out of necessity we quickly learned to duck. The five pound hymn book landed below on top of a devout old lady. She screamed the whole congregation into chaos while jumping around like a chicken without a head. The following Sunday the parish priest urged my father (from the pulpit) to stay after mass for a small chat. My father's friend needled him afterwards over a glass of beer, "What did he want, what did he say?" It's about my boy Peacock," he answered. I wished I could make a disappearing act but no I had to offer my bum once again. Families did not sit together in the church pews. The men sat at the right and the women sat at the left. The oldest at the far back and the youngest at the front. Teenagers became cross-eyed. The only reprieve came at the offering and at the communion. Then they could straighten out the eyes again. For the offering the whole congregation starting with the oldest men filed around the altar. Everybody made the trip. No one dared not to. Those with money dropped it in a container at the side of the altar and those without money or those who pretended not to have money just dipped their finger into the container to rattle the coins as proof of their giving.

To be able to receive communion one was requested total abstinence from food and drink starting at midnight. That posed serious problems especially during cold winter days. Occasionally people fainted and crashed between the pews. It was cruel. Vatican Two somewhat eased the requirement: one hour abstinence before receiving communion. On my first communion day I tasted the communion cake before heading to church. Of course nobody knew it except God. He did not thunder bolted me to the ground so it must have been alright for Him.

The Sacrament of the Eucharist

The Catholic Church believes that in the Holy Eucharist the body, blood, spirit and divinity of Christ, the God-Man, are truly and substantially present under the appearances of bread and wine. This presence of the entire Christ is by reason of the transubstantiation of the bread and wine into the body and blood of Christ, which is accomplished in the unbloody sacrifice of the Mass. Jesus Himself instituted the Eucharist and requested its repetition (Luke 22:19–20).

The sacrament of the Eucharist is a true sacrifice, a representation of the sacrifice of Christ on the cross, for the ritual elements of the sacrifice are identical with the body and blood of Christ (Hebrews 9:12,14).

The Eucharist is a sacrament of unity. It is meant to unite the faithful more closely each day with God and with one another.

When a priest pronounces the words of Eucharistic consecration, the underlying reality of bread and wine is changed into the body and blood of Christ, given to us in sacrifice. That change has been given the name of 'transubstantiation'. This means that Christ Himself, true God and true

Man, is really and substantially present, in a mysterious way, under the appearances of bread and wine.

The sacrifice of the Mass is not merely a ritual that commemorates a past sacrifice. In it, through the ministry of priests, Christ perpetuates the sacrifice of the cross in an unbloody manner. At the same time, the Eucharist is a meal that recalls the Last Supper, celebrates our unity together in Christ and anticipates the messianic banquet of the kingdom. In the Eucharist, Jesus nourishes Christians with His own self, the Bread of Life, so that they may become a people more acceptable to God and filled with greater love of God and others.

> Jesus said to them, "I tell you the truth, unless you eat the flesh of the Son of Man and drink his blood, you have no life in you. Whoever eats my flesh and drinks my blood has eternal life, and I will raise him up at the last day. For my flesh is real food and my blood is real drink. Whoever eats my flesh and drinks my blood remains in me, and I in him" (John 6:53–56 NIV).

Most Protestant denominations do not celebrate the Eucharist as mass. They took, however, one of the main three parts from it, so that their services are centered around that part: the Liturgy of the Word. From the Liturgy of the Eucharist, they retained the money offering, the tithe. Luther's theory called consubstantiation, the existence of God's presence in the Eucharist, was that the body and blood of Jesus Christ coexisted with the substances of bread and wine. Again, it is in strong contrast to the Catholic view of transubstantiation, that the sacramental bread and wine change into the body and blood of Jesus Christ when consecrated during the mass. Many Protestants, while taking communion, declare that they take the symbols of His body and blood: bread and wine. Jesus' words, in Matthew 26:26–28, clear the controversy.

> While they were eating, Jesus took bread, gave thanks and broke it, and gave it to his disciples, saying, "Take and eat; this is my body." Then he took the cup, gave thanks and offered it to them, saying, "Drink from it, all of you. This is my blood of the covenant, which is poured out for many for the forgiveness of sins." (NIV).

Jesus did not say, "This is the symbol of my body" nor "the symbol of my blood," but "this is my body ... this is my blood." It is the spiritual, which is unseen, manifested in the natural, material, which is seen.

The Eucharist is the sacrament of love, the love Jesus Christ has for all humanity. It is represented by His Sacred Heart. The worship and reparation to Christ for men's ingratitude, manifested particularly by indifference to the Holy Eucharist, is directed to the person of Jesus Christ Himself.

Growing up Pains and Joys

My parents were convinced by allowing me to be part of the local boy scouts would further my Christian upbringing. The parish priest paid for our uniforms, the tents and everything one could imagine boy scouts may need. He was very proud of us and we were not going to deceive him at an upcoming Jamboree. In fact our troupe won the first price in building the camp site. We mastered a wooden fence, benches, tables and a grandiose entrance gate. All was handcrafted with freshly felled evergreen trees (teenage trees). Basically we clear cut one and a half acre of pine evergreen forest. The local farmer did not mind if we picked up the fallen fruits in his orchards. We gave the fruit trees a good shake to enhance our harvest. Camp fire potatoes are delicious especially organized ones (we stole the potatoes from the farmers' fields but called it organizing). All went extremely well at the Jamboree, we, boy scouts, had just a wonderful time. The parish priest was so proud of us till the forester came on the scene to the forest which was no more. The parish priest bailed us out, he was our spiritual leader and the incident never made it to the newspapers.

I was the third in line to be the first born. My brother Pedro is three years older than me and my sister Margot is two years older than me. They are not only older than me but they are also taller than me. Normally we were well behaved except for a dozen times per week we had to fight, push, punch and give each other new names. Not so much with our sister than with Pedro. He nicknamed me Gustav Simon (Gauleiter) and I returned the favor by calling him Kratzenberg. Both were German occupation officials hated by everybody. One fight stands out to this very day and the result is still written in my face, even after so many years. We haggled over a ball pen. He first pushed me than I pushed him after that he took a swing at my face specifically my nose. I saw blood, grabbed a butcher knife and threw it at him. The knife missed his toes by centimeters. Next I threw my jam sandwich at him, again I missed but the sandwich did not miss the new drapes nor the new wallpaper. In desperation I left the house. A 'free range' chicken caught my attention. I tried to pen it again but was that chicken every dumb. I picked up a stone and threw it at the chicken. By now I had practice, the stone killed the chicken. Slowly my anger and frustration wore off giving rise to apprehension and fear: fear of my mother. Surely this time I headed for a spanking. So many wrongs never make a right. I got an idea. Protection was the answer for my troubles. I cut a piece of sheet metal to fit my bum and stuffed it in my pants. I could face anything now even my irate mother. My mother came home from shopping to hear the litany of all my crimes. Kratzenberg was the divulger. Sternly mother called me. This time I did not run off but bravely presented my behind. "Boing, boing!!" followed by a deep silence. My mother noticed my sheet metal claded bum and broke out in laughter. I was saved. In any case when you laugh you have no strength to do anything else. My nose was not so lucky. Painful and red swollen it begged for furious attention. Icepacks somehow eased the pain and the swelling a little bit. Weeks later my doctor spoke the verdict, "The nose is broken, it mended itself already but as you can see it is crooked. We have to wait until you are adult. Then come and see me again. I will break the nose again and straighten it out." I never went back. Who wants his nose broken even when it is crooked. By the way it adds to my features. Doctors are like that. Recently I noticed a lump in my throat. My general practitioner (doctors always practice on you hence practice of doctor so and so) send me to a throat specialist who in turn send me to five other throat specialists all in the same building and on the same floor. In the end they all came together and proudly announced, "We all agree we do not know what it is." Next I was send to a throat surgeon. Many tests were performed on me at the General Hospital. I was assured in six weeks they would have a diagnosis. You can imagining how worried I was. In my desperation I asked a health food store clerk, "Do you have anything for a lump like this?" "Not to worry about it, it is just chicken fat, "she replied. I insisted, "What do you mean by just chicken fat?"

"When you skin a chicken there is slight yellow fat under the skin and that's what you have." I remembered I was eating a lot of veal at that time not chicken.

The growth hormones fed to the calves were the culprit not the chicken. Feeling better already I left and waited for my appointment with the throat surgeon. When he greeted me he was all smiles and said, "Not to worry about it, it is just chicken fat. If you want it removed give me a call when you are ready and I will cut your throat (his exact words)." No thanks, nobody is going to cut Peacock's throat as long as he has a say in it.

Our parents taught us foremost by example, good examples and sometimes examples how not to do it. Here is one such example. Our parents did not swear nor did they use scientific (fowl) language. Occasionally our father, while hammering around the house, targeted one of his fingers. It could be either the left or the right hand because he was multi-dexterous. You could never predict which finger from which hand he would hit (hammer). When he hammered his finger he screamed, "Ush" spiced with scientific language. My mother would scold him, "Johann how can you say this things in front of the children". He would reply, "I can not say 'Our Father who is in heaven' I am too angry. You do not talk to God when you are that angry." My brother Lion would mock our father. One of our cousins was named 'Ush'. "Dad would you like me to get cousin Ush?" Our father smoked only one or two cigarettes per week and only on Sundays while walking with his children in the forests. He was a man of few words, words he readily distorted on purpose. It always kept my mother going. In fact it drove her up the wall. I inherited the same trait from my father. It keeps my wife going. Lately I noticed that she distorts words too, what an achievement on my part. Men do not want women to change (always like the wedding day, eternally beautiful) but women want men to change (the character). Sometimes women deteriorate over night.

Our father was one of a kind. He worked in a steel fabricating plant (1200 workers). He was the only one to start work one hour sooner than anybody else and he also went home one hour sooner. He convinced his superiors that it is good to come to a warm office in the morning (he volunteered to made fire in the oven that heated the office). The real reason to get home an hour sooner was to look after the animals: cows, pigs, rabbits, chicken and his children. One Sunday he failed to look after the rabbits. His friends told him about a Hawaiian movie, a must see. He left in a hurry Sunday afternoon to meet with his friends in the movie theatre. My mom was miffed, she knew the movie was not so much about Hawaii (landscape) than girls (bodyscapes). Before he left he fed the rabbits but forgot to close the cage of the mother rabbit and her offspring. The cat seized the opportunity. Later in the afternoon my mother found eight little rabbits mauled to death. She was resourceful and prepared a perfect rabbit meal. By the time my father returned from the movie my mother presented him the rabbit dish saying, "Hawaiian delight" (the title of the movie). It was delicious, far better than the meal my aunt's husband presented to my father. He sold him a cow. A week later he pedaled forty kilometers to receive payment. The brother-in-law invited my father for diner, diner he had already prepared in advance. The physical exercise had sharpened his appetite. He just wolfed down the meal in no time. He was in a hurry to return home but the brother-in-law insisted to show him the pelt of the animal he just ate. My father thought he ate a rabbit. In reality he ate a dog. What a disappointment, he never sold a cow to the deceiver.

I do not know how other people dress themselves. My father was very particular in dressing for church Sunday morning. He started from top to bottom. As soon as he had the shirt and the tie on he put the hat on and finished downwards Seeing him in underwear with the hat already on looked clowny.

My father was the boss outside the home, my mother was the boss inside the home. She loved her children. Babies made her happier than anything else. She shielded us from any danger, sometimes that meant from our father who had a much shorter fuse to burn than our mother. Even today I wonder how our father could run that fast. I suppose once his fuse was burnt he rocketed in my direction. In my despair I run to my mother for cover. She would shield her little Peacock and forgave him almost anything. I hated school, I had more important things to do because I could not faint sickness, instead I told my mother the teacher is sick, no school today. By the way if you are sick or pretend to be sick you had to stay in bed. I was found out when the neighbor's daughter came home from school brandishing her schoolbag.

Up to nine years of age I always had supper by sitting on the lap of my mother. That was my comfort place (safer too, out of reach of my father's hat with which he would hit me when I was naughty). Then my brother Fred was on the way. My mother's tummy got so big, there was no room left for me anymore. I moved to the right of my father, straight in the line of fire (the hat). I had better behave. Fred arrived on Sunday (he likes Sundays the best). Fred was born in the maternity clinic. Our father went to see mother and little Fred in the afternoon. Pedro, the one who broke my nose, Margot our sister and myself ought to go to church for vesper service. Pedro and myself we did not have vesper in mind but celebration and celebrating we did. As soon as Margot left for church we jumped into action. Our father made his very own wine from red currents. One thing we noticed whenever he drank some of the stuff he became so jolly we wanted to become jolly too. We filled a big cooking pot with red wine and drank straight from the pot. We figured the least utensil we used the least we had to clean and wipe any trace away from our drinking binge. Slowly the wine took affect. There are three stages in getting drunk. First stage you act like a monkey (funny) second stage you become like a lion (strength) and third stage you behave indecently like a pig. We passed first stage quickly and started quarreling accusing each other of drinking too big sips. More drinking, the furniture moved around, the kitchen table landed on the stove, the chairs fell over and so did we. We made it out of the house, fell to the ground and everything was turning. We both rolled down the driveway beside the house, rolled over the highway and landed in the opposite ditch. No car drove over us (angels protected us), the ditch was dry. We passed out before stage three kicked in. Margot found both of us in the ditch, thinking that we both were driven over by a truck and that we were dead. She cried profusely, ran to the house. There she realized the truth. She grabbed a broom and broomed us back into the house. We promised her heaven and hell just do not tell mom and dad. She promised, tucked us into bed and removed any trace. When dad came home she told him, "Pedro and Peacock are not feeling well but they will be alright. That was the end of it, or so we thought. Anytime Margot wanted something (blackmail) she got it for years to come, just for keeping mousey about it. Finally we broke the curse over us by telling our mother what had happen that day.

Fred grew quickly. By the time he was four he stumbled around a lot. Our parents were quiet worried until they found out the source of the balance problem. The little rascal siphoned the wine barrel a couple of times a day; he was jolly too like our dad. Two ladies from the neighboring village dropped in one afternoon. Both suffered from a very bad cold. Our dad suggested a few glasses of his homemade red wine. They agreed, it may cheer them up a little. When they left our home they were already jolly. On their way home they got lost in the forest where they wandered around for hours. Totally exhausted they finally reached their home. After a good night sleep they woke up. The cold was gone. Now they wondered how they made it home in the first place.

The Gift of the Holy Spirit

Peacock reached the age when Catholics are confirmed: an important step in the life of any Christian. The sacrament of confirmation is the gift of the Holy Spirit. It is the sacrament of Christian maturity.

Confirmation or Baptism of the Holy Spirit

Catholics and Protestants differ in the way they confer this sacrament.

The Protestant Way

The person must love Jesus. The proof of that love is obedience to what He commands. "If you love me, you will obey what I command. And I will ask the Father, and he will give you another Counselor to be with you forever—the Spirit of truth" (John 14:15–17 NIV).

"We are witnesses of these things, and so is the Holy Spirit, whom God has given to those who obey Him" (Acts 5:32 NIV).

When these two conditions are fulfilled, nothing stands in the way for you to receive the Holy Spirit. All you have to do is ask your heavenly Father.

The Holy Spirit is a gift. "And you will receive the gift of the Holy Spirit. The promise is for you and your children and for all who are far off—for all whom the Lord our God will call" (Acts 2:38–39 NIV).

The giving of the Holy Spirit to a person is a sign of acceptance by God of that person. "God who knows the heart, showed that he accepted them by giving the Holy Spirit to them, just as he did to us" (Acts 15:8 NIV).

"I [John the Baptist] baptize you with water, but he [Jesus] will baptize you with the Holy Spirit" (Mark 1:8 NIV).

It is Jesus who baptizes you with the Holy Spirit. You ask the Father, and Jesus will, by the laying on of hands, baptize you with the Holy Spirit, through His established spiritual authority in your area or your surroundings. That authority may be your local pastor, a visiting evangelist or any Spirit-filled believer. A believer who does not know the Holy Spirit cannot give what he himself does not have. God is not restricted in His ways as to how to give the Holy Spirit. At times blowing or breathing on a person has the same results.

"Then Peter and John placed their hands on them, and they received the Holy Spirit" (Acts 8:17 NIV).

"Again Jesus said, 'Peace be with you! As the Father has sent me, I am sending you.' And with that He breathed on them and said, 'Receive the Holy Spirit' (John 20:21–22 NIV).

To baptize means to dip, to plunge or to immerse. In regards to baptizing with the Holy Spirit it means to pour out or to pour over. So the Holy Spirit is poured on or poured over a person.

The Catholic Way

The Holy Spirit is given to a baptized believer by anointing him or her with chrism (a sanctified mixture of oil and balsam) in the form of a cross on the forehead, the imposition of hands and saying the words, "[Name], receive the seal of the Holy Spirit, the Gift of the Father."

Regardless which way is chosen the effects are tremendous. The confirmed person receives the Holy Spirit in a special way, and from then on he or she does well to have a close relationship with the Holy Spirit. The gifts of the Holy Spirit are also given, at least some of the gifts. Unfortunately most people neglect the Holy Spirit and very few operate in the gifts of the Holy Spirit. A great boldness to evangelize and to profess one's faith is a sure sign of the Holy Spirit's divine influence. The bishop is the ordinary minister of confirmation, or there can be an extraordinary minister, a priest for instance, to whom the power has been granted by office or by apostolic indult as an exception.

The Gifts of the Holy Spirit

A gift is freely given. You do not pay for it, you do not work for it and often you do not deserve it. There are spiritual and natural gifts; they do not compete with each other but complement each other. The gifts of the Holy Spirit find their field of operation in the six-fold ministry, namely: the ministry of helps, the ministry of the apostles, the ministry of the prophets, the ministry of the evangelists, the ministry of the pastors and the ministry of the teachers. These ministries are gifts by themselves. One could compare the six-fold ministry to an army with the Holy Spirit as the high command, the apostles, evangelists and prophets as the officers, the pastors and teachers as the sous-officers and the ministry of helps as the troops. As a believer you are part of the troops. A soldier does not take vacations, nor can he desert his post. If he does, he will be shot. Are you, the believer, still at your post, or did you take a permanent vacation? If you are still at your post, are you armed and equipped properly? If you do not put on your spiritual armor, you are naked, and if you do not operate in the gifts of the Spirit, you do not carry any weapons either. Pray that the enemy will laugh himself to death when seeing you.

> "It was he who gave some to be apostles, some to be prophets,
> some to be evangelists, and some to be pastors and teachers,
> to prepare God's people for works of service, [the ministry of

helps] so that the body of Christ may be built up until we all reach unity in the faith and in the knowledge of the Son of God and become mature, attaining to the whole measure of the fullness of Christ" (Ephesians 4:11–13 NIV).

Every person is called by God to serve, nevertheless few are chosen. The calling is universal, but the choosing depends on you. You must fulfill certain conditions for God to choose you.

The ministry of helps is, number wise, the most important ministry. Actually, billions of people should be in this ministry worldwide. In comparison, it is equal to the ministry of the apostle, the prophet, the evangelist, the pastor and the teacher. The bulk of the work is accomplished by the ministry of helps. It is the workhorse, the backbone, so to speak. Without it, very little can be achieved by the others.

"He who receives you receives me, and he who receives me receives the one who sent me. Anyone who receives a prophet because he is a prophet will receive a prophet's reward, and anyone who receives a righteous man because he is a righteous man will receive a righteous man's reward. And if anyone gives even a cup of cold water to one of these little ones because he is my disciple, I tell you the truth, he will certainly not lose his reward" (Matthew 10:40–42 NIV).

This makes it clear; in God's eyes if you work in the ministry of helps for an evangelist you will receive an evangelist's reward. The ministry of helps is active in your family, your work place, your community, your local church and all of the ministries of the apostle, the prophet, the evangelist, the pastor and teacher. Many will stay in the ministry of helps for life; few will be chosen by God to the other ministries as the Holy Spirit sees fit. While active in the ministry of helps, you are being pruned, hammered on the anvil, into a useful believer and worker. It is a time of heart circumcision, a time of character building. Out of the ministry of helps come the apostle, the prophet, the evangelist, the pastor and the teacher. The importance of the ministry of helps cannot be overemphasized. It is here where the training takes place. If you desire to become a pastor and are not active in the ministry of helps, you are fooling yourself. You may be a pastor but a dead one, a thimble Christian at best.

"So Elijah went from there and found Elisha son of Shaphat. He was plowing with twelve yoke of oxen, and he himself was driving the twelfth pair. Elijah went up to him and threw his cloak around him" (1 Kings 19:19 NIV).

> So he asked Jesse, "Are these all the sons you have?"
> "There is still the youngest," Jesse answered, "but he is tending the sheep."
> Samuel said, "Send for him; we will not sit down until he arrives."
> So he sent and had him brought in. He was ruddy, with a fine appearance and handsome features.
> Then the Lord said, "Rise and anoint him; he is the one" (1 Samuel 16:11–12 NIV).

"Now Jesus himself was about thirty years old when he began his ministry" (Luke 3:23 NIV). This clearly indicates Jesus was involved in the ministry of helps for at least eighteen years prior to his full-time ministry. Nowadays we call the ministry of helps ministry in the marketplace, the place where you have influence as a housewife, as a worker, as a politician, etc. Jesus was obedient to His earthly parents (Luke 2:51 NIV) and even more so to His heavenly Father. "Didn't you know I had to be in my Father's house?" (Luke 2:49 NIV). One can conclude with certainty that Jesus was active in the marketplace of His days, which prepared Him for His teaching ministry that culminated in his crucifixion and resurrection.

The gifts are given to witness to the people and to build the church, the bride of Christ.

> There are different kinds of gifts, but the same Spirit. There are different kinds of service, but the same Lord. There are different kinds of working, but the same God works all of them in all men. Now to each one the manifestation of the Spirit is given for the common good. To one there is given through the Spirit the message of wisdom, to another the message of knowledge by means of the same Spirit, to another faith by the same Spirit, to another gifts of healing by that one Spirit, to another miraculous powers, to another prophecy, to another distinguishing between spirits, to another speaking in different kinds of tongues, and to still another the interpretation of tongues. All these are the work of one and the same Spirit, and he gives them to each one, just as he determines" (1 Corinthians 12:4–11 NIV).

The revelation gifts are wisdom, knowledge and discerning of spirits. The power gifts are faith, healing and miracles. The vocal gifts are tongues, interpretation of tongues and prophecy.

The gift of wisdom is an instruction to a person or persons for the present or for the future in relation to marriage, family, friends, job, ministry, finances, relationships, health, etc., to avoid disaster, to come out of a difficult situation or to make excellent and to build up. It can be for your body, mind or spirit.

The gift of knowledge is a message to a person or persons from the past or from the present. It can be something that the person does not know, like a disease or sickness, or something that the person knows, like having had an abortion in the past. The gift of knowledge is not to expose a person but to bring that person to a place where the Holy Spirit or Jesus can touch him or her.

The discerning of spirits is a gift enabling a person to distinguish between good and evil spirits. It is a badly needed gift today. Many so called Christians attack the work of the Holy Spirit, thinking it is from the devil. On the other hand, they believe doctrines taught by demons. This gift also enables you to know what spirit you are dealing with, like a lying spirit, a deceiving spirit, etc.

The gift of faith is different from the measure of faith that every human being received. Your measure of faith enables you to operate in faith, in God's mode of operation, while the gift of faith is a power set into motion for a person who is unable to activate his own measure of faith. Remember nothing happens in the spiritual realm unless faith is present; it is the way God operates.

The gift of healing, through it a person is healed (from sickness and disease) in his body, mind or spirit.

The gift of miracles supersedes the natural laws. For instance, you have only one leg and a new leg grows, you have no eyes and a pair of eyes is created in your eye sockets, you are in a fierce fire but you come out not a hair singed or a person may be dead but that person can be brought back to life. There is no limit to the gift of miracles.

The gift of tongues is plural because there are different modalities of tongues. You speak in tongues, your spiritual language, to God, or while speaking in tongues, a person or persons hear you speak in their native language. Other times you speak in your native language and a person or persons hear you in their native language.

Speaking in Tongues

Every born of God believer has a spiritual language. Unfortunately most of them are mute because they do not know that they have a spiritual language. Their language is inactive and dormant. The spiritual language is called speaking in tongues. "All of them were filled with the Holy Spirit and began to speak in other tongues as the Spirit enabled them" (Acts 2:4 NIV). For anyone who speaks in a tongue does not speak to men but to God. Indeed, no one understands him; he utters mysteries with his spirit and his mind (physical mind) is unfruitful. No two believers utter the same words; it is as personal as your fingerprints.

To understand the spiritual language, one must comprehend the basic principle of how God's word works. The written word of God, contained in the Bible and lying on the shelf, accomplishes nothing. But when that word is spoken by a believer (whose heart operates in faith and who acts in the authority of Jesus) that word is endued with power, activated and accomplishes what it is supposed to accomplish. Life and death are in the power of the tongue.

The spiritual language is a gift of the Holy Spirit. It is He who guides you, enables you and puts power into your speaking. The spiritual language must be spoken by your physical body to cause a spiritual or natural event to occur, to change its course or to prevent it from happening in the spiritual or natural realm. Why do we have to speak it? Because we, as humans, are in authority here on earth.

Speaking in tongues is like sending out a carrier wave, and the Holy Spirit is superimposing the characteristics of signals onto that carrier wave and directing it to where it is supposed to go, and it will accomplish its task. The good thing about this is we will not get in God's way and Satan and his demons cannot listen in. Here are but a few examples of what speaking in tongues does, but keep in mind God is not limited unless we limit Him.

When you speak in tongues you are speaking divine mysteries "...he utters mysteries with his spirit" (1 Corinthians 14:2 NIV). What are those mysteries?

"...we speak of God's secret wisdom, a wisdom that has been hidden and that God destined for our glory before time began" (1 Corinthians 2:7 NIV). In the Bible, the wisdom of God often refers to the plan of God on the earth. It keeps God's plans concealed from the enemy, Satan. Keeping the devil in the dark about what God is doing is very important.

1 Corinthians 2:8 illustrates this very well. "None of the rulers of this age understood it, for if they had, they would not have crucified the Lord of Glory" (NIV).

As you pray in tongues, secrets will be revealed to you, Spirit to spirit. You are praying God's plan for your life, for the life of others, for the implementation of God's Kingdom here on the earth and for the destruction of Satan's work.

> We have not received the spirit of the world but the Spirit who is from God, that we may understand what God has freely given us. This is what we speak [in tongues], not in words taught us by human wisdom but in words taught by the Spirit, expressing spiritual truths in spiritual words (1 Corinthians 2:12–13 NIV).

When you don't know what or how you should pray, tongues are the answer. If you don't have sufficient knowledge or information in order to pray intelligently, you can pray in the Spirit, confident that He will pray through you. "In the same way, the Spirit helps us in our weakness [inability]. We do not know what we ought to pray for, but the Spirit himself intercedes for us with groans that words cannot express" (Romans 8:26 NIV).

Refreshing, edifying or re-strengthening is yet another facet of speaking in tongues.

> Very well then, with foreign lips and strange tongues God will speak to his people, to whom he said, "This is the resting place, let the weary rest"; and, "This is the place of repose"—but they would not listen (Isaiah 28:11–12 NIV).

"He who speaks in a tongue edifies himself" (1 Corinthians 14:4 NIV).

By now you may wonder, "How do I get started?" Speaking or praying in tongues is an act of your will. God does not and will not override your will. You are a free person and you must take the initiative if you are going to speak in tongues. Too many people think the Holy Spirit will suddenly pounce on them and take control of their vocal cords. This is not how God operates. You don't have to try all kinds of things either. Here is how you go about it. Ask for the gift of tongues and then take the initiative.

Start praying, but not in words that you understand. Simply exercise your will to make an utterance and allow the Holy Spirit to shape it. The

Holy Spirit will develop your prayer language as you yield your body to Him, as you submit your mind to Him and as you surrender your spirit to Him. At the back of your mind you may think "This is just me, I am making this up." Of course it is you. It is your spirit being spoken to and through by the Holy Spirit. The proof of the Holy Spirit's involvement comes as you are edified, built up and refreshed. You will know then that it's not just you.

The interpretation of tongues occurs when you speak in your spiritual language and another person translates your spiritual language into a human language such as French, English, etc.

The gift of prophecy is a message to a person or persons for the future and is usually conditional. God always reveals the future to his people.

If you are a full-time minister, all the gifts should be operational in your life. The best gift is the one needed in a particular situation at a specific time. Function determines structure. If you do not use the gifts they become non-operational.

"For God's gifts and his call are irrevocable" (Romans 11:29 NIV). God does not take his gifts back or withdraw the calling on your life, but through your fault and wrong choices, the gifts may become non-operational and it is up to you to follow God's calling.

The gifts are for the common good, not for your prestige or for your financial gain. Any believer should eagerly desire the gifts of the Holy Spirit and put himself in a position to receive those gifts. Nevertheless, there are some conditions to be fulfilled to be a candidate. You must be able to yield your body, submit your mind and surrender your spirit to the Holy Spirit. You must put your natural gifts to good use in the service of others. If those natural gifts are buried, how can you expect the Holy Spirit to give you spiritual gifts when you are a bad steward of your natural gifts and talents?

The Holy Spirit is the great orchestra for God's saving plan of mankind. He gives the gifts to different people to do specific tasks. It is not for us to pick out some field of service and then ask the Holy Spirit to qualify us for that service. It is not for us to select some gifts and ask the Holy Spirit to impart to us these self-chosen gifts except for the gift of tongues. The gift of tongues is different from all other gifts in that it is for every believer who has received the Holy Spirit. But you still have to ask for it. It is up to us to simply put ourselves at the disposal of the Holy Spirit to send us where He wills, to select for us what kind of service He wills and to impart to us what gift(s) He wills.

"God also testified to it by signs, bold wonders and various miracles, and gifts of the Holy Spirit distributed according to his will" (Hebrews 2:4 NIV).

The Holy Spirit Speaks to You. Are You Listening?

One thing is certain—the Holy Spirit speaks to us, but, unfortunately, we do not hear Him, or we hear Him seldom. The culprit is not the Holy Spirit; rather we are the ones who neglect to listen. He speaks to us in more than one way. We are spirits. As such He speaks to our spirits even though we may hear or perceive Him in the natural realm.

The Holy Spirit comes to us when we are quiet. That does not necessarily imply a quietness away from the world or an isolated place where you are totally alone and where complete absence of noise exists. These things may help but are not a prerequisite. I am talking about an inner quietness. You may be busy, noise may surround you, but you operate with an inner peace where your inner conversation is not overpowering the still small voice of the Holy Spirit. The Holy Spirit has twenty-four hours a day access to you to speak to you. Are you ready? We may not hear Him, and we may blame others for it, but mostly we are to be blamed for not listening and not hearing.

The Holy Spirit speaks to you in different ways. Most of the time it is through the Word of God. He will bring to remembrance a certain verse or paragraph and give you revelation through it. Other times, while you are reading the Bible, suddenly a verse jumps out at you and takes on a whole new meaning you never noticed before. Or the Holy Spirit speaks through the Word of God while a preacher or any person proclaims the Word.

He speaks to you through your conscience. Each time you come close to Him, or when you start praying, He reminds you of the thing or things in your life that are not right. He wants you to change them before you can have a loving relationship with Him.

He speaks to you, to your spirit, any time of the day or night, no matter in what situation you may find yourself.

"The Spirit told Philip, 'Go to that chariot and stay near it'" (Acts 8:29 NIV).

He speaks to you through a natural event or occurrence. At one time, I was thinking about a certain situation in my life, which was very bothersome, and wondering how to handle it. While thinking about it I zipped my jacket; at that very moment, the Holy Spirit spoke to my spirit, "Zip your mouth." It turned out to be the best advice.

He speaks to you through visions, which are mental images. People may talk to you in those visions. Visions happen while you are awake, not to be confused with hallucinations.

He speaks to you through other persons. Often those persons are not even aware that the Holy Spirit is ministering to you through them.

At times, He may use your mouth and tongue to speak to you audibly and loudly to get your attention quickly. You may be in the process of doing something very foolishly or bad and the Holy Spirit wants to prevent that, so He gets your attention immediately. "...for it will not be you speaking, but the Spirit of your Father speaking through you" (Matthew 10:20 NIV).

He may make use of an animal to speak to you. In the Old Testament the story of Balaam shows us the diversity by which the Holy Spirit speaks to us human beings. Obviously Balaam did not listen to God, so God used a donkey to get his attention. "Then the Lord opened the donkey's mouth, and she said to Balaam, 'What have I done to you to make you beat me these three times?'" (Numbers 22:28 NIV). Read the whole chapter; it will make you laugh; God has the greatest sense of humor. The closest I ever came to an event where an animal and the Holy Spirit were involved is the following true story, which happened in 1995. I was on my way to a certain address to do electrical work. No matter how hard I tried to find the place, I could not. I found the house with the number next to the number where I was supposed to work. So I decided to knock at that door and ask for it. The front yard was fenced in with a small door, leading straight to the house. I entered and closed the door behind me and walked towards the entrance. Three steps were leading to the house door, which was open. I was about to engage the first step when a fierce pit bull flew through the open door at me. There was no escape. I raised my arm to ward off the dog, but the next thing I noticed he was hanging with his clenched, strong jaws on my left wrist. Suddenly, I started barking fiercely at the wild animal. Stunned, he let go, looked at me in disbelief, turned around, tail between his legs and disappeared into the house. The owner came out, asked what I wanted, told me the neighbor was half a mile away because of the funny shape of the road. I did not tell him about the dog, in fact I was trespassing. What good would it have done? Under the influence of the Holy Spirit, my mouth was barking at the opportune time to save me from being torn into pieces. Even my wrist was unharmed—not even a scratch. The dog's teeth marks can still be seen today on my wristwatch's metal bracelet. Possibly, I was barking in a language understandable by the dog. There are situations where there is no time for the Holy Spirit to speak to you. He just will take over.

We, myself, my wife and my daughter, were driving in our family car to the local shopping mall. As usual, my wife prayed in tongues in the back seat. Out of the blue, the car in front of us stopped abruptly. At that very moment someone (the Holy Spirit) took over the steering wheel. For the next ten seconds that steering wheel turned rapidly several revolutions to the right then to the left and again to the right. I became the observer and not the doer. Miracle-like, the car fitted in an empty slot between the fast moving traffic in the other lane. I also noticed the horrified people on the sidewalk. They threw their arms up in the air, opened their mouths to scream, and then when nothing happened, closed their mouths again without uttering a single sound. Everything turned to normal again: no accident, no scratch and no sound, thanks to the Holy Spirit.

Often we do not hear the Holy Spirit, because our mind and body get in the way. So He uses times and methods when our mind and/or our body are out of order.

While we speak in tongues, the Holy Spirit speaks to our spirit. "This is what we speak, not in words taught us by human wisdom but in words taught by the Spirit, expressing spiritual truths in spiritual words" (1 Corinthians 2:13 NIV).

You may be slain in the Spirit. While you are slain in the Spirit you fall under the power of God. The power of God is so immense, no one can stand in His presence and survive unless God shields and protects him. God uses only as much power as is needed to overcome our resistance and to accomplish what He wants to accomplish. Many times, when God wants to heal you, to anoint you, to speak to you, to impart a spiritual gift to you, to bathe you in His presence, to love you and so forth or even to give you directions, He slays you: you fall under His power. You may find yourself in a charged atmosphere where God's presence is so thick, so rich and tangible, you just crumble and fall on the floor.

Often we put up resistance, our mind becomes a hindrance to what God wants to do. Falling under His power partly suspends our physical senses and bypasses our mind, so that God can easily act on our spirit. When you are slain in the Spirit your physical body and your mind are practically out of order, but your spirit becomes acutely aware and sensitive to the things of the spirit. You become numb to your surroundings, your physical senses are dulled but your spiritual senses are greatly sharpened.

Paul, the apostle, on his way to Damascus, fell under the power of God. "As he neared Damascus on his journey, suddenly a light from heaven flashed around him. He fell to the ground and heard a voice say to him, "Saul, Saul, why do you persecute me?" (Acts 9:3 NIV).

The Holy Spirit speaks to you through dreams while you are asleep. He wakes you up in the middle of the night, not fully, but just enough that your spirit is fully aware, but your mind and body are still drunk with sleep. Many times the Holy Spirit speaks to me just prior to waking up in the morning. In the minute timeframe between sleep and wakefulness, He is able to speak to me without me getting in His way.

Listening and hearing the Holy Spirit is not enough, you must respond to Him, and that response should always turn into action. Real communication is never a monologue.

Kurwalden: a Vacation in the Swiss'Alps

Six months vacation in the Swiss' Alps is exciting. But the reason to get to that point was anything but exciting. It actually was a disaster. At the new parish priest's inauguration, a Swiss tourist, a rich Swiss tourist, rammed his car into the crowds. "Brake failure," he claimed. My sister Margot was one of the victims. She had pleaded with our mother not to go, but our mother was firm and made her go. Six months after the accident the Swiss tourist offered my sister a vacation in the Swiss Alps (her leg was healed by then). Our parents never thought of suing the tourist but they readily accepted the offer under one condition: Peacock had to be invited too. I was told that I had to keep an eye on my sister. My suspicion was that our parents needed a break from me and that my sister had to keep an eye on me instead. The resort town of Kurwalden, nestled among snow covered mountains, exceeded my expectations. .

There were about eighty children, most of them had real health problems like asthma. Those children hardly gave any problem to the caregivers. It was those who had no health problems (like me and another fellow called Tom) who were the problem. Tom was one year older than me. He was such a nice guy who helped me a lot to get into trouble. It is good to have a friend like that, then life is much more interesting and never boring.

We all had to take a two hour nap every day or almost everyday. For Tom and myself that was asking too much. We rather roamed around and explored things. One of the places to explore was the ladies' washroom. When everybody was napping we sneaked into the washroom. We hardly checked things out when two of the lady caregivers entered the washroom. It was not just a washroom but there were some shower stalls there too. We huddled in one of the toilets with the door ajar. The two ladies (young) started taking off their clothes. They peeled off one piece after another till they were stark naked. One proceeded to take a shower, the other came towards the toilet stall where we were gasping. God did a superb job in creating women. Adam and Eve wore no clothing till they messed up. The caregiver opened the door, our door. She screamed and ran for cover, we ran for safety. Later, they caught up with us and we were called on the carpet. Their faces were hard as the wooden floor we were standing on. "What do you have to say for your defense?" one peeped. "We used the ladies' washroom, which is further away from the dormitory so that we would not flush the children out of their nap."(that was a solid lie sin for confession). Their facial expressions relaxed somehow, they believed us. It must have been our contrite faces. Tom and myself we knew that it was a big lie, the kind you need for confession. We were not given physical punishment nor were we dubbed peeping Toms. We had to write five hundred lines, "We shall never use the ladies' washroom." How boring that can be! So I wrote, "Girls are beautiful." It was shorter too. The stern look on the caregiver's face made me quickly fall in line again writing the punishing lines. However I detected a faint smile under her uncompromising demeanor.

Many of the children were under the age of seven. They did not read yet. So the caregivers would read everybody's mail during meal times. At times they became all excited laughing and having the best of time. Margot, my sister, and I we knew we had mail from home. Our mother was an interesting storyteller which came handy for our oldest brother Pedro. He refused to please the teacher at all cost, so he did not study, he disliked the teacher with passion. Our mother wrote his essays most of the time. While handing back the essay, the teacher would say, "An "A" for your mother."

We all enjoyed our stay in Kurwalden. For one thing there was no real school, instead a lot of roaming the wintry forests and snow covered mountains. To the end of the six months we climbed a bigger mountain. For the occasion I wore my best suit. We reached the peak at 3 P.M.. We all marveled at the gorgeous scenery. One sour note to our excursion: it took us to long to climb to the top. Therefore we had to glide down the mountain but not with sleighs. We reached the bottom just when the sun died down. By then some of us were bottomless. Leather pants took on a new meaning. The gliding down was too much for my Sunday pants. Yesterday's newspaper had to fill in the gap and cover the red cheeks. I wondered how I could return home in a few days? The caregivers were kind enough to stitch a patch on my beige pants. They probably did not have a great selection for the patch or they just took revenge. The patch was a blushing fire red. I looked like a clown. In the train home I mostly kept seated but I still had to face my mother. We were so glad to be reunited again. I kept my back against the wall at all times and was moving sideward. My mom finally said, "Peacock what's the matter with you, you act so funny, turn around. Reluctantly I did. There was the red patch. My mother broke out in laughter. She had humor and I had worried all the time for nothing, what a waste of energy.

Boarding School

To me it was a mixed blessing to pass the college admission test. I had to give up my freedom of roaming around. The college was a boarding school in Belgium. The whole estate was boarded up by fifteen feet high stone walls with an iron gate usually closed shut. The students were told that it was meant to keep intruders out but we had strong suspicions that it was meant to keep us in. Up to that point my grades were dismal at best. Sorry to say it I had no choice in the matter anymore. Everybody had to study for hours, I mean hours every day. There was no escape to it. Every minute was structured with strictly enforced silence sprinkled throughout the day, and during the night no peep at all. No wonder everybody did his best to break the monotony. I wished there would have been 'her best' as well but it was a boys only school.

I knew I could not sing, not even do, re, mi…but I excelled in every other aspect of the music course. In fact I was the best in class. My classmates begged the professor numerous times that we should practice singing and that I, as the best of the class, should sing first. You guessed, it was a disaster with the whole class holding their sides (including the professor) from laughing. The racket was so turbulent that the principal showed up wondering what the commotion was all about.

There were twins in the class. I could not distinguish one from the other neither could anybody else tell them apart. They dressed the same, had the same hair style and above all both were very mischievous. They knew how to take advantage of their twin hood and seized any opportunity to engage in naughty pranks. Of course they would get caught, that was just part of the game. The wrong twin usually would get punished. After a while no professor dared to discipline them for fear they would slap the innocent one (but we all knew both were guilty most of the time). One professor's duty included the title of disciplinarian of which he proudly made use of. We called him, "the enforcer". By the time we made it to the breakfast table we were all starved. Like hungry wolves we fell over the plates, stacked with slices of bread. One student had the misfortune to grab the whole plate. He tried to put most of the slices back on the plate but the enforcer prevented him from doing so. "You take it you eat it," he grinned. Poor fellow he had to gorge himself with eighteen slices of bread. What a pity full sight. While tears ran down his cheeks he kept munching and munching till the stack disappeared through his mouth. His stomach became extended to the point of great discomfort and pain.

During breakfast, silence was strictly enforced. Every student had to take turns to read from a book, most of the time a true story. I was reading about an old lady and how she got murdered. That was the wrong time and place to get the giggles. I got the giggles and there was nothing nor anyone who could stop me not even the enforcer and his threats. I survived the ordeal (the laughter).

The end of the semester quickly approached. One more week of slave work (exam) and we all would go home for a three week vacation. Before we left for home, the exam results were made public. Those with good marks enjoyed the vacation and those with bad marks were hunted by them. How cruel! When I heard about my marks I thought there must be a mistake. I was the first of my class with the highest marks in every discipline. I never expected that. Now the pressure was on to perform in the future. My parents felt that their Peacock was good for something after all. Nevertheless I did not last in college. Three years in boarding school took their toll on me, physically speaking. I became very sick. The doctor was called to examine me. His diagnoses sealed his faith not mine. After pronouncing a death sentence over me (three to six months to live) he died of lung cancer. I quit college and studying altogether, went home and roamed the forests again. In the end I did not kicked the bucket but was left with a heart condition. A heart condition I quickly forgot the name still to this very day. In that way I do not tell anybody the name so no one can pronounce the disorder over me. It was common practice to drug the students in boarding schools. The reason was to make the enforcer's task easier, no consideration was given to the health nor the rights of the students. Sounds familiar; just think of the residential schools. My parents took me to a new doctor, a young doctor, a heart specialist. He gave me strong heart medication that almost did me in but I had no choice if I wanted to improve. The new heart doctor performed an abortion on his young wife. It nearly killed her. She never forgave him for the butchery (his father was a butcher).While the patients were in the waiting room the temperaments of doctor and wife flared up. They screamed and threw obscenities at each other. I learned to duck. He gave me hardly any hope and that sealed his faith too. I left yet for another doctor. The last I heard from the doctor and his angry wife was eight months later. I was working as an apprentice across his practice (in the offices of the E.U. courts). By now they did not scream anymore they were shouting full blast. Four months later this young doctor (34 years of age) fell victim to liver cancer. I realized when a doctor put you down it will put him down for good. My new doctor also a heart specialist was very pleasant. He gave me great hope. His diagnosis was that I should take medication for a few months, and then get a job. You must work physically, your heart requires that then you will be totally alright. Each time he looked at my heart (he had his own x-ray machine in his office). At that time all doctors practiced from their residences. It gave you a good feeling. The setting was often in the midst of a beautiful and peaceful garden. He also told me about his vacations in Canada British Columbia. He mentioned Vancouver with all its natural beauties. Little did I know at the time that I would spend most of my life in that part of the world. His diagnosis was right. A few months later I became an electrician apprentice and no more medication.

Apprentices are a breed of their own, especially in Europe. They do not get pay but they receive pocket money for the bus etc.. You receive seven cents per hour for the first year, twelve cents for the second year and thirty cents for the third year. The emphasis is placed on learning and not on making money. It was still better than my parents' generation. They had to pay the employer to learn a trade.

All my experiences as an apprentice had to do with drinking alcohol in excess. There was this fellow worker who got regularly into drinking while on the job. He was the one who attended the coal-fire heating system of the company's building. When drank he would retire to the coal pit (where it was very hot) and sleep the drunkenness off. Nobody minded him as long as he kept to himself but that was often not the case. When jolly and a little bit more he would verbally abuse his co-workers. A thin piece of plywood spiked with tiny nails placed in his sandwich did not stop the abuse. The co-workers patience ran out. They grabbed him, dragged him to the workshop, cuffed his left sleeve in a wise and his right sleeve in another wise. All the while he was shouting obscenities at the workers. Then came the hard liquor treatment. He was force fed with it. Soon his tongue quieted down, he was ready for the coal pit. That incident cured him miraculously.

Peer pressure was everywhere. Normally I did not drink any alcohol. The people from Luxembourg eat a lot, drink a lot therefore use the toilets a lot. I was challenged by my work team to drink with them or else. I bought the best wine (eighteen per cent alcohol) to show them that I was not a 'chicken' after all. I slurped the whole bottle down in no time and in no time I passed out. We worked at a hotel and our material and equipment was stored in one of the hotel rooms, that's were it all happened. Eight hours later (the work shift was over) I came to myself. I have no recollection whatsoever. Apparently my co-workers took me to the Red District. I supposedly amused the patrons for hours in those establishments (prostitution is legal in Luxembourg). Everybody knew that I was a Catholic (Cat-holic in opposition to dog-holic). For that reason the foreman selected me to work in brothels and the bishop residence. The later almost proved fatal. Luxembourg is entirely built on caves and tunnels. During lunch time a co-worker and myself ventured into those dark, gloomy caves and tunnels. Armed with only one tiny flashlight we accessed the underground world through the bishop's wine cellar. At the beginning everything unfolded according to plan. Some of the tunnels were so narrow you had to crawl on hands and knees. From time to time we encountered deep holes filled with water. You fall in, you drown. We were about to return when the flashlight died on us. My co-worker panicked. Instantly he became tunnel phobic and I was scared to death. Constantly I had to reassure him. There was no time to waste, we had to find our way out of the maze of tunnels, caves and holes. It is amazing how quickly one becomes the best friend of God and verbalizing promises one never dared even to think about before. Nobody knew we were in the tunnels, for other people we just vanished. Four hours later we re-emerged in the wine cellar too shaken up to uncork any bottle of wine even though we badly needed a drink. Three years of apprenticeship past quickly. There were more jobs than workers, so employers offered high wages even before you hinted you may leave the company. My boss was no exception. He promised me one third above regular journeyman wages if I would stick around. He knew I was drafted to the army for a compulsory one year.

Army Life

Within months army training can make you physically fit. There were no female soldiers in the Luxembourger army at that time. Being deprived of any female company for months took its toll on all of us. Many portrait clear homosexual tendencies in their behavior. Humans are not meant to be segregated in male only or female only. It's not healthy for the well being of spirit, mind and body. The officers realized the problem and took action by bringing girly show to the barracks (Strictly for your eyes only). Many soldiers selected the more masculine looking girls as their favorites and only a few selected the real feminine girls. Furthermore the army command saw the real need for married soldiers to get a weekly pass to see their wives and children. The sexual orientation in humans is a learned function. The following paragraphs will shed some light on the controversial subject of homosexuality.

Homosexuality

Talk about homosexuality, and you have people reacting in the most unconventional ways. Scorned by society, gays and lesbians stood in the shadow for centuries. Our twentieth century's liberality brought them out of the closet and into the limelight. When AIDS came on the scene, and the majority of infected people were homosexuals, they were beaten and bashed and often deprived of their basic human rights as human beings and citizens. That was wrong then and still is today. People of all walks of life have been infected with AIDS since then, so the shame and abuse have somewhat eased a little.

We hear a lot about homosexual rights. The homosexual community does not talk about basic human rights but about the right to be homosexual, to get married with a same sex partner, to have the same benefits as normal couples, from the state and from the church. It is abnormal to be homosexual and those rights should never be granted to them, neither by any state nor by any church.

Jesus Christ died for every one of us regardless of our sexual orientation. He did not come into the world to condemn us but to save us. God the

Father sent His only Son Jesus Christ out of love for us all. Homosexuals should not be scorned nor put to shame but loved in the true Christian sense. God does not hate but loves everybody. God hates sin, and every human being should hate sin. Some people think there is no sin and everything that feels good one should do. Others say, "Live by your conscience; you choose; whatever you choose is right." Our conscience is meant to be a safeguard, some kind of last resort and ultimate authority in dealing with our inner self. But, for many, that conscience is weak, polluted and deceived and no longer fulfills the task it is supposed to fulfill. Only if your conscience confirms it with the Holy Spirit, can you rely on it. You must be led, guided and taught by the Holy Spirit on a continual basis, day by day.

What is sin? Sin is a transgression of a natural or spiritual law affecting or harming your body, mind or spirit and/or the body, mind or spirit of other persons. Homosexual activities are sins; it is a transgression of a natural and spiritual law set forth by God Himself. It is unnatural to have sexual relations between two men or two women; it is a sterile undertaking and there can be no fruitfulness whatsoever.

When civil authorities approve of a so called 'marriage' between two parties of the same sex, they show their lack of understanding of what marriage is all about. It is mind boggling to see the same politicians and leaders being deceived and blinded to such a degree that what is wrong becomes right and what is right becomes wrong.

There are times when governments reward people for breaking natural or spiritual laws. Take abortion for instance. Killing of offspring is against natural and spiritual laws and yet blinded government officials provide physicians and funds for women to get it done. If 100 percent of the people say it is all right, that still does not make a wrong right.

Many homosexuals, counselors and even doctors say, "Gays and lesbians are born that way; there is nothing that can be done". That's a lie, a cop-out and a cheap excuse not to do anything or even to try to change. It is similar to parents who think their child's intelligence is solely determined by heredity. So if a child is born a dummy, he or she will always be a dummy. Nothing could be further from the truth. What determines a child's intelligence depends on the first six years of appropriate, specific stimulation to neurologically organize that child's brain. The result will be a very high I.Q.

Animals come into the world with their structures much more organized to function in almost rigid patterns. Their nervous systems are more complete and the patterns of connections directing activity are almost set and unalterable, but fit for early action. Human beings are born with a tremendous part of their nervous mass unpatterned, unconnected, so that people, depending on where they may happen to have been born, can organize their brains to fit the demands of their surroundings. Man's brain can learn to do in many ways what animals can do only in one fixed way. I repeat, no one is born a gay, a lesbian or a heterosexual. The sexual orientation is a learned function for the human species.

Some say, "There is no cure" Cure is a wrong term because homosexuality is not a disease nor a sickness but an acquired result from a learned faulty mode of doing things, actions repeated innumerable times for years on end, which mold the physical, mental and spiritual body. It takes three weeks to form a habit, and it takes three weeks to break a habit. Homosexuality can be changed, it can be reversed and a normal, healthy way of expressing one's sexuality can be learned. Yes, homosexuals can be completely delivered and set free and become heterosexual through and through.

Because homosexuality is a learned function, to reverse it depends entirely on the individual. Some individuals either do not want to change or do not know how to change or do not know that they can be changed. In a free society, where everybody is entitled to their opinion, the populace at large does not necessarily always opt for the truth but rather what the trend is and often the easy way out. Those so-called educated people, who are misinformed, misled and blind to the truth, who ought to be a guiding light for the less educated, come up with same sex parenting as a valid topic for children's books. During their formative years, preschoolers and first-graders are brainwashed to believe "male moms" and "female dads" are normal. Universities, giving courses along those lines, violate their God-given right as a teaching and educational tool for the public at large. Children of all ages are lured to believe a lie, they are deceived and we, as adults, carry the blame.

Reasons That May Cause Someone To Become A Homosexual Rather Than A Heterosexual

#1. Sexuality as such and all its behaviors are learned functions. Nobody is born a homosexual. To be a homosexual is the sum total of all interior and exterior environmental influences. At the onset, nobody wants to be homosexual but is drawn into it because of lack of knowledge and a sincere desire to do something to correct a wrong sexual behavior pattern.

#2. Our sexuality is fashioned right from birth. Parents, or the lack of parents, have a great influence on children's development. The first six years of a child's life are the most significant for that child's development. A loving family environment is the basis of all normal sexual maturity.

#3. Sexual abuse and molestation by a parent, a brother, a sister, a relative, a friend, a teacher or any other person will often have a dramatic effect on the young child and may wreck and destroy that child's sexual development for life.

#4. A wrong, sterile social environment created by our society will promote homosexuality. Children, teenagers, and adults: all are influenced by it. I call it segregation of the sexes: boarding schools for boys only, boarding schools for girls only, the army (all male or all female), the jails and even religious institutions. There are companies that employ only men and others which employ only women.

All those environments leave a trail of homosexual abuse behind. Not only the child and the young adult but even the adult, the teacher, the superior, all are prone more than in any other social setting to become abnormal in their sexual orientation.

#5. Sexual repression. The sexual drive and the propagation of the species are amongst the strongest drives in human beings. False and erroneous education, as well as a stern repression of that drive, in most cases causes a reversal of sexual orientation. The beautiful sex drive is now destructive, centered on self, and to affirm itself looks for expression in the same sex. Parents, teachers and educators bear a tremendous responsibility to teach the truth through words and actions by being themselves models to their pupils. Sex is neither dirty nor sinful but finds it fulfillment in a loving marriage.

#6. Hormonal influences are often unknown and neglected, yet we all depend on the proper hormones, male or female. The adrenal cortex produces both: male and female hormones in both sexes. However, the main production of sex hormones is secreted by the testes in the male and by the ovaries in the female. Small amounts of the sex hormones of the opposite sex are produced by the adrenal cortex in both sexes. Normally, those hormones are not powerful enough to cause masculinization in the female or femininization in the male. About two percent of sex hormones of the opposite sex are present in a normal man or woman.

The adrenal androgen (male sex hormone) is of physiological significance in females, who otherwise lack androgens. It is responsible for androgen-dependent processes in the female, such as growth of pubic and axillary hair, enhancement of the pubertal growth spurt and development and maintenance of the female sex drive. In the male the active intra-cellular androgen is responsible for development of the prostate and bulbourethral glands as well as the seminal vesicles.

Male and female hormones can be out of proportion in either sex, which can lead to a "liking" of a same sex person, and those persons may display the secondary sex characteristics of the opposite sex.

#7. Lack of proper exposure to the opposite sex is very important in early childhood and teenage years. A girl growing up without the father takes on a masculine image and a boy growing up without the father around becomes effeminate; he takes on the character of the mother. If the mother is missing, proper development is also hampered; love's ability is affected.

Hormones affect men and women, not only when taken orally but also through the skin or just by being in close proximity. Men who extracted estrogen from the urine of pregnant mares and those working to produce drugs (estrogen, progesterone, etc..) became impotent and developed breast tissue. Some doctors prescribe patches to supplement extra estrogen for menopausal women. A patch is applied to the skin and the patch releases a small amount of synthetic estrogen in a continuous way. It flows from the patch to the skin to the blood. A male environment is able to influence menses and ovulation in women exposed to that environment, and a female environment will bring about a synchronization in the menstruation habits of the women exposed to that environment like mother and daughter, office workers, etc.. The hormones of a person exercise a regulatory affect on the opposite sex, living in close proximity. A widow, who has lost her male companion, often displays a hormonal imbalance.

For a man to stay sexually healthy, he must be exposed to a female, and for a woman to stay sexually healthy, she must be exposed to a male and for boys and girls to develop properly they must be exposed to both males and females. The family is that ideal environment. Spend some quality time with your wife, your husband and your children.

#8. Spiritual influence. As spiritual beings, we are all influenced either by the Holy Spirit or by evil spirits. Our enemy, an evil spirit or the devil, loves and delights to see human beings get off track, especially in sexual matters, because the destruction can be complete and lasting and often involves more than one person.

They exchanged the truth of God for a lie, and worshiped and served created things rather than the Creator—who is forever praised. Because of this [worshiping created things rather than God, which is idolatry] God gave them over to shameful lusts. Even their women exchanged natural relations for unnatural ones [lesbians]. In the same way the men also abandoned natural relations with women and were inflamed with lust for one another [gays]. Men committed indecent acts with other men, and received in themselves the due penalty for their perversion (Romans 1:25–27 NIV).

I have mentioned eight reasons why a person may have become a homosexual. Every homosexual is influenced by evil spirits; if that were not the case they would not be homosexual because to be influenced by the Holy Spirit excludes homosexuality. All other reasons are contributing factors only. Any of those factors do not necessarily influence a person to become a homosexual. Most people lack a clear understanding of what causes homosexuality and therefore if they are gay or lesbian they accept the fact; I should say accept the lie, that nothing can be done. If you are sincere, and you want with your whole being to become a normal person in respect to sexual orientation then the next paragraph is for you.

What Can I Do To Become A Normal Heterosexual?

Sexuality as well as homosexuality involve your total being—spirit, mind and body. To be successful you must address all three areas of your human nature.

Spirit

- Have a loving, personal relationship with God the Father, God the Son and God the Holy Spirit. Let the Holy Spirit lead, guide and teach you day by day.
- Feed your spirit with spiritual food, which is the word of God: the Bible.
- Forgive anybody who may have done wrong to you in any area of your life.
- Speak victory and not defeat.
- Ask God to change you, to heal you, to deliver and set you free from the bondage of homosexuality.

Mind

Learn how to control yourself through your mind. Receive everything, including your homosexual desires, but do not accept them; rather redirect them through assumption towards your new goal.

Use visualization as a re-educative tool. If you have a spouse of the opposite sex, he or she can be of great help to you.

Sexual gratification caused by stimulation by the same sex partner, male to male or female to female, will soon become a habit (21 days) and the object of sex, I should say the target person, will in the future be directed exclusively to that same sex partner. Sexual stimulation aided by thoughts, feelings and imagination will translate into acts and actions.

Something is only sexual in the measure it activates the sexual cerebral structure and the awareness or consciousness. If a sexual message or a thought that is homosexual is taken in a different way by the brain, it ceases to be homosexual and no longer has any homosexual power.

Awareness gives us the capacity for judgment, differentiation, generalization, the capacity for abstract thoughts, imagination and so forth. The delay between thought and action is the basis of awareness. Think first, then act.

The delay between a thought process and its translation into action is long enough to make it possible to inhibit it. This possibility of creating the image of an action and then delaying its execution, postponing it or preventing it altogether is the basis of imagination and intellectual judgment.

Learn the beauty of the opposite sex. Look forward to meeting new friends and people of the opposite sex. If you were mistreated or abused by someone of the opposite sex remember there are a lot of good people of both sexes around.

Learn how the brain functions, and choose an appropriate mode of action.

Body

Change your environment, quit your homosexual friends, and let them know you are changing. Sometimes it demands quitting your job, finding a new place to live or moving to another city or town. Start anew.

Whatever you do, make sure you find yourself in a mixed environment, men and women, and positively look out for the beauty in the physiology and psychology of the opposite sex.

See a doctor to find out if your male and female hormones are in the right proportions. The liver converts testosterone and androgen from adrenal source to androsterone and etiocholanolone; both are excreted in the urine. The ratio of androsterone to etiocholanolone can be used to discriminate between heterosexuals and homosexuals. Homosexuals excrete less androsterone than etiocholanolone, while heterosexual males secrete more androsterone than etiocholanolone.

Do a development test on yourself. (Refer to the book "HOW TO AND WHEN" published by Holy Fire Publishing) If you fail in any of the levels and stages, do the appropriate exercises regardless of your age, to reprogram your brain.

When we learn a new task, we seldom succeed the first time. A child who learns to walk, falls more than once, but he or she gets up and continues and after a while walks perfectly. So if you do not succeed every day, do not be discouraged but continue diligently, and you will be successful. As a man thinks, so he is, so think highly of yourself no matter what your shortcomings. We all have different talents and I.Q.'s. What is required from us is to work diligently and not to give up. I personally prefer someone who works hard, who has little talent, than someone who works little with a lot of talent.

Remember a single person is not complete, it takes A and B, a man and a woman to be complete. Two A's or two B's by themselves do not make a complete entity and never will make a marriage either. Make the right choice; it is in your power. Your well-being—spirit, mind and body—depend on that choice.

Army Exploits

Eight months of rigorous training completed the initial service. During those times we were the ones to perform honor guard duties for foreign heads of state visiting Luxembourg. Thailand's Queen Sirikit was honor guarded by my company four hours in the blazing sun. Some of us passed out while on duty. They stood too rigid and collapsed.

I was relocated close to my parents' home for the remaining four months of army service. The duties assigned to me and other electricians were to maintain and repair field telephones, scramblers and decoders. Plenty of free time provoked us to build a switching centre for field telephones. A hobby we all enjoyed. Bribe infiltrated our ranks. I managed two weekly evening passes (six PM to ten PM). Apart from those semi-legal passes we also climbed the compound fence to visit the local pubs where go go girls performed. The barely dressed girls did not incite me to heavy drinking. I barely drank at all to the irritation of my soldier comrades. The chicken syndrome popped up again. I had no chance to ferret out of it. The time and place were agreed on: the next day was the day after the last call of the MP. (10 P.M.). My opponent was a sturdy, heavy set, athletic drinker. I had to use ruse to win this one. The challenge was who of us two could drink the most without getting stoned. I opted for hard liquor only, the other fellow drank a mixture of wine, beer and hard liquor. We drank so much we lost count of it. I visited the washroom a lot. The strategy was not to swallow but to spit it either in a handkerchief or in the washroom sink. It worked perfectly. Nobody suspected fowl play because it is normal to use the washroom when you drink a lot. By two AM my drinking partner slumped in his seat. I was the winner, time to head back to the army compound. I had to carry the guy for a twenty minute walk. We waited nervously in the bushes to see the MP make their rounds then I clawed up the fifteen foot fence with the monkey (hundred eighty pounder) on my back. On top I dropped him among bushes to soften the fall. I knew the timing of the guards very well. We waited for the next round to pass then we hurried to the dormitory (two flights of stairs). All of them were wondering if we would ever make it back. By then it was already two in the morning. It took some huffing and puffing before we reached the dormitory door which I kicked open with one foot. I held the monkey by the scup of the neck and with the other hand the center of gravity which was his pants. I swung him a few times to get momentum then threw him inside on the floor. Instantly I became an undisputed hero. I kept the booze title till I was discharged with honor. My superior officer wanted to make a career army officer out of me but I rejoiced in leaving army life behind for good.

I came to a crossroad in my life. Was life senseless? If not what was the meaning of it? Were all people railroaded in their thinking? You are born, you grow up, get a job, make money, get married have children and die. It was not a very good outlook. That cycle repeats itself over and over again like a broken record. Take my best friend for instance. He proposed to my girl friend (the one I undressed as a child). My girlfriend did not like him but when she saw him so dejected, she had pity on him and said yes. They had a few children together but she was never very happy. To marry someone pity does not cut it you must love that person with all your heart and soul. The girl's mother told me afterwards, "We pay the price for being proud". My father was a laborer but my boyfriend's father was a teacher (the one who threw square rulers at you). Years earlier the teacher came to our home for civic enumeration. My mother mentioned that I would go to the seashore for an all paid vacation by the social services (I did not grow enough compared to my peers). When time came my parents were told there is no room for your son but the teacher's son went instead (influence peddling). Many of those children who went were very sick. My boyfriend came back, sick too, he contracted tuberculoses of the spine. It was a blessing that I did not go. God so many times protected me, the rascal. I still cherish the countless hours we spend together in total childhood freedom, innocence and contentment. It hurts the most when the closest friends to you betray you. Our friendship withered from that time on.

Yes, there was more to life. There was God, building His kingdom and the prospect of everlasting life: eternal life. So life was not in vain after all. I wish parents and teachers would draw their children and pupils' attention to the supernatural aspect of human life. There can never be a conflict between the natural and the supernatural, between the physical nature and the spiritual nature, between the divine and the secular. God does not make a separation between the two. They are inseparable, all part of the human being: spirit, mind and body. I passionately wanted to know God so I decided to become a Catholic monk. My mother was opposed to the idea. She rather wanted me to marry and have some little 'Peacocks'. Months later my mother reported about a girl who cried out her eyes for six weeks after learning that I was in the monastery. We never talked to each other. A few times we smiled at each other. Smiles are stronger than words. They say. "I approve of you, I like you and possibly I love you." She was very beautiful and charming.

Dr. Peacock goes to the Monastery

It makes sense to enter monastic life if you are serious to know God. Not just knowing about God but to get to know God in the deepest sense of relationship. Monks are the professionals, they dabbled for centuries in God's affairs. Even professionals encounter pitfalls. It is very dangerous to think of yourself as knowing all. It hinders you from going forward and reaching new heights. And then there is the calling of God for every human being. God has a destiny and a purpose for each and every one. No one is born by chance. God knows the beginning and the end. Everybody is called to build God's kingdom. We are all in it, there is no room for a lone ranger. Some are called to be a parent, a father, a mother, a teacher, a monk, a priest, a minister, a doctor, a fireman, a policeman, a tradesman, a nurse, an accountant, a farmer, a miner, a pilot and the list goes on. There are multitudes of callings to serve each other with the ultimate goal to know God. Monks should be free from daily worries: food, drink, clothing and shelter. Every monk and nun commits him or herself to at least three vows: chastity, obedience and poverty. Some orders have a fourth vow: location. They stay for life at the same location, no travel, staycation at best. Basically there are two kinds of monastic life to choose from or being called to (there goes the choosing).

Both phases should be part of every Christian's life. For a true mature Christian, operating in love must become a way of life. Some Christians may primarily operate in Phase One (Mary), others in Phase Two (Martha), but all should operate to some extent in both phases.

> As Jesus and his disciples were on their way, he came to a village where a woman named Martha opened her home to him. She had a sister called Mary, who sat at the Lord's feet listening to what he said. But Martha was distracted by all the preparations that had to be made. She came to him and asked, "Lord, don't you care that my sister has left me to do the work by myself?' Tell her to help me!"
>
> "Martha, Martha," the Lord answered, "you are worried and upset about many things, but only one thing is needed. Mary has chosen what is better, and it will not taken away from her" (Luke 10:38–41 NIV).

Martha and Mary illustrate both phases perfectly.

God calls dedicated men and women to implement His redemptive work among people. Some are like Martha, others like Mary. The Sisters of Mother Teresa of Calcutta operate in both Phases. The Sisterhood of Mary, a Protestant women's order, operates primarily in Phase One. There are so-called active orders of men and women and contemplative orders of men and women. Contemplative orders encourage their members to seek union and communion with God through love but by seclusion and freedom from the worldly spirit, thus the objective worship of God is perfected. In purpose, it is a continuous life of prayer to God that His kingdom may flourish and dying to oneself in consolation to Jesus Christ for reparation of the many people who not only neglect to worship God but through their lifestyle greatly sadden Him. They wipe the tears of Jesus in solitude and silence.

On the other hand, there is the active apostolate, which must rely on the contemplative apostolate to be of any success. Romans 12:4 tells us that not all members have the same function. Most missionary orders are active orders. They build churches, schools, hospitals, etc. to implement a social structure in which they can impact the local population and win them for Jesus Christ.

There is a Catholic order I became a member of. It is called: The Fathers of the Sacred Heart of Jesus. It is partly a contemplative and partly an active apostolate including missionary work. It stresses the worship of Jesus for His love represented by His heart. The worship is centered on reparation to Christ for men's ingratitude manifested particularly by indifference to the Holy Eucharist. The worship is not directed to the heart alone but to the person of Jesus Christ.

There is a twelve months preparation period prior of becoming a monk. Three months of postulant followed by nine months of novice under the guidance of the novice master. At that time there were too few applicants in Luxembourg so the applicants from Luxembourg, Belgium and France were potted together in France in the city of Amiens. Altogether we hardly made it to twenty. Many of our friends and relatives thought we were insane although it might do us some good. The day to enter the monastery arrived quickly. I hardly could wait to see the location. The monastery nestled among high trees in a rural area, one hour walk from Amiens. The whole complex was surrounded by high brick walls. I knew instantly they were to keep us in not to keep intruders out. Thieves do not run to monasteries to rob. Soon we met each other. There was one Congolese applicant by the name of Leblanc (the white one) and one from France with the name of Lenoir (the black one). How confusing that can be. I found out what made Leblanc excited. When we were arguing or quarreling among us I shouted, "Mangez-vous." (meaning devour yourselves). Leblanc came from a cannibalistic tribe, hence the excitement. In a monastery you need any help you can get to fight boredom. The total structuring of the days and nights can made you loose your marbles. Humoristic events are vital for your mental health.

Preparation time is basically a time of taming yourself. Once you tamed yourself you can tame others. This holds true for marriages as well. Unless you tamed yourself do not try to tame your spouse. This is the reason number one for divorce. Another meaning for taming yourself is becoming holy, holy as in holiness. You tame your temperament, your wants, your desires, your choices. You will be no longer affected what people think or say about you, good or bad, and you will have great power and authority.

The first step is dying to yourself. It does not happen over night, it is a process, a life-long process for some.

Dying to Oneself

Before anything substantial can happen in your walk with God, you must die to yourself; you must decrease and Jesus must increase. The conditions for dying to yourself are summed up in three words: yield, submit and surrender, in that order. They are synonyms with a difference.

First you yield your body to the Holy Spirit. Yielding means giving way with an implication of compliance. You do not yield to temptation, but you yield to the Holy Spirit. The desires of your physical body do not control you anymore, but you control them. You must "offer your bodies as living sacrifices, holy and pleasing to God" (Romans 12:1 NIV).

You must submit your mind to the Holy Spirit. Submitting means giving up all resistance and giving in to the power, the will or authority of another.

"Do not conform any longer to the pattern of this world, but be transformed by the renewing of your mind" (Romans 12:2 NIV). You renew your mind so that it conforms to the Word of God and to the influence of the Holy Spirit. You stay in control of your decisions and your choices.

"The seventy-two returned with joy and said, 'Lord, even the demons submit to us in your name'" (Luke 10:17 NIV). Demons never surrender to anybody.

"...the sinful mind is hostile to God. It does not submit to God's law, nor can it do so" (Romans 8:7 NIV).

"Now as the church submits to Christ [not surrender], so also wives should submit to their husbands in everything" (Ephesians 5:24 NIV). God does not delight in a surrendered church but a submitted church. Many husbands confuse submit with surrender and force their will down the throat of their wives, and they have the gall to use God's Word to back up their demands.

"Submit yourselves, then, to God. Resist the devil, and he will flee from you" (James 4:7 NIV). Again this verse emphasizes submit and not surrender.

You must surrender your spirit to the Holy Spirit. Surrendering means giving up control or possession and is always preceded by a struggle, a resistance or a fight. Your spirit is the real you. Before you are able to surrender you must first die to yourself, not a physical death but a spiritual death. This spiritual death is not to be confused with the dead spirit of an unborn-again person. Dying to yourself does not come easily. Dying to yourself starts with your physical body; next is your mind and then your spirit.

"They are not of the world, even as I am not of it" (John 17:16 NIV).

"I have been crucified with Christ and I no longer live, but Christ lives in me" (Galatians 2:20 NIV).

First of all, after you have died to yourself, you are no longer of the world; you are crucified with Christ and no longer live, but Christ lives in you.

"And when Jesus had cried out again in a loud voice, he gave up [surrendered] his spirit" (Matthew 27:50 NIV).

"Jesus called out in a loud voice, 'Father, into your hands I commit [surrender] my spirit'" (Luke 23:46 NIV).

"They said to the Ammonites, 'Tomorrow we will surrender to you, and you can do to us whatever seems good to you'" (1 Samuel 11:10 NIV).

God looks for yielded vessels (bodies), submitted minds and surrendered spirits. God does not want your minds surrendered but submitted. He created you a free person; he is not glorified by zombies. Some people surrender their body, their mind and their spirit to the devil. They will be totally possessed by evil spirits. After they kill a person or persons or commit other gruesome atrocities, they say, "The devil made me do it." They forget that the devil has only as much power over them as they allow him to have.

We find a very good example of yielding, submitting and surrendering in Genesis 32:22–31 (NIV).

> That night Jacob got up and took his two wives, his two maidservants and his eleven sons and crossed the ford of the Jabbok. After he had sent them across the stream, he sent over all his possessions. So Jacob was left alone, and a man wrestled with him till daybreak. When the man saw that he could not overpower him, he touched the socket of Jacob's hip so that his hip was wrenched as he wrestled with the man. Then the man said, "Let me go, for it is daybreak."
>
> But Jacob replied, "I will not let you go unless you bless me."
>
> The man asked him, "What is your name?"
>
> "Jacob," he answered.

Then the man said, "Your name will no longer be Jacob, but Israel, because you have struggled with God and with men and have overcome."

Jacob said, "Please tell me your name."

But he replied, "Why do you ask my name?" Then he blessed him there.

So Jacob called the place Peniel, saying, "It is because I saw God face to face, and yet my life was spared."

The sun rose above him as he passed Peniel, and he was limping because of his hip."

To die to yourself you have to get up and move from where you are to a new location. You unsettle yourself, the way you think, the way you do things. Jacob detached himself from his wives, his servants and his sons; the most precious persons in his life. Jesus says in Matthew 10:37 (NIV), "Anyone who loves his father or mother more than me is not worthy of me; anyone who loves his son or daughter more than me is not worthy of me."

Then Jacob detached himself from all material possessions. Material things will keep you bound and captive unless you release them to God. If they are your treasures, God cannot be part of you. "For where your treasure is, there your heart will be also" (Matthew 6:21 NIV). Jacob was left alone—no one and nothing stayed with him.

Dying to yourself, you must do it by yourself. It is a struggle between you and God. Without God, there will be no struggle, and there will be no dying either. It is a time of darkness, at least that's the way it is perceived by human nature. You struggle till you have victory over yourself, till daybreak. That daybreak may come in days, years or in a lifetime, it's up to you.

"When the man saw that he could not overpower him, he touched the socket of Jacob's hip so that his hip was wrenched as he wrestled with the man" (Genesis 32:25 NIV). At first this seems controversial, you may ask yourself why God Almighty could not overpower Jacob. Before Jacob was able to yield his body to God, God had to touch him. Only then was Jacob in a state to yield his body. The other noteworthy point is God does not go against your will; He will never overpower you. You must submit your mind to Him.

Our body and mind are not made perfect the minute we are born-again; a thorn in the flesh is given us, which stays with us as long as we live here on earth. To understand a thorn in the flesh, let's see what Paul the Apostle had to say about it.

> To keep me from becoming conceited because of these surpassingly great revelations, there was given me a thorn in my flesh, a messenger of Satan, to torment me. Three times I pleaded with the Lord to take it away from me. But He said to me, "My grace is sufficient for you, for my power is made perfect in weakness" (2 Corinthians 12:7–9 NIV).

A thorn in the flesh can be anything that is not perfect, not of God. It is the consequence of the fall of Adam and Eve: insults, hardships, persecutions, sickness, disease, difficulties, weaknesses, etc. They are all messengers of Satan. We can turn the thorns in the flesh into beautiful roses by dying to ourselves in yielding our body and submitting our mind to God. "I will not let you go unless you bless me" This speaks of a submitted mind, not a surrendered mind. Jacob let God touch him then hung onto God and request He bless him. And God blessed him. But not only that, He also changed him, from Jacob to Israel, from supplanter (Up to then he always took hold of the possessions of others: his brother's birthright, his father's blessings, his father-in-law's flocks and herds.) to Israel, prince with God.

It is so important to understand the difference between submitting and surrendering, yet most if not all dictionaries list them as synonyms. Here is a natural example: You see a dentist. You yield your body, more specifically your mouth and teeth to him. He suggests that you need a tooth pulled, you agree, you allow him to do it; you submit your will (mind) to him. Then he suggests he hypnotize you so you will feel no pain. You agree again; he hypnotizes you; you surrendered your will, your mind to him; he can do with you whatever he likes to do; you have no say in it anymore.

The only time a person should surrender to another person is among spouses. To reach total loving communion in the act of lovemaking, both husband and wife have to yield their bodies, submit their minds and surrender their spirits to each other. And they will be one in body, mind and spirit. Often only their bodies are yielded; no loving communion is taking place, no oneness and no likeness in the image of God.

Dying to yourself, yielding your body, submitting your mind and surrendering your spirit is not a one-time occurrence but a constant process and it produces the right priorities in your life.

Raising your arms and hands to the Lord is a physical sign of surrendering, an outward sign. You are in the most vulnerable position there is. This outward sign should be preceded by an inner yielding of your body, a submitting of your mind and a surrendering of your spirit. Some people criticize the falling under the power of God or the way it is produced or initiated like the laying on of hands, blowing on you, etc. We should not criticize the working of the Holy Spirit. The main thing is that a particular person is touched by God, healed in his or her physical body, restored, set free from any bondage, blessed with God's spiritual gifts but most of all blessed with God's presence and love.

While lying on the ground, under the power of God, you may experience all kinds of physical manifestations. Some people weep uncontrollably, others shake or feel a numbness but almost all the time you feel total peace, you are wrapped in a blanket of God's love and the warmth of God's presence surrounds you. I say 'God' because it could be Jesus, the Holy Spirit or the Father. Your spiritual senses are greatly sharpened; you see clearly; it makes it easier for you to see the truth and to live by the truth.

God may speak to you (your spirit) and give you specific instructions and guidelines: things you must change, people you must forgive or work He wants you to do. It is all part of your loving Father nurturing you, sustaining you and bringing you to maturity. How intense and rewarding your experience is, is up to you. It is your choice to bring to fulfillment what is imparted to you by the Most High.

Monastic Life

For the first few weeks the learning of the routine kept us busy. Every segment of the day was initiated by the ringing of a two foot bell. At the first bell sound we were supposed to stop talking or to start talking what ever we were doing at that time. That can be tricky when you stop in the middle of a sentence or continue of an old sentence (word economy). A civil cook and his dog (not a monk) prepared all meals for the monks. The dog knew when to behave and when not to behave. The dog run off with the roast of the day just when the bell rang to silence everybody. One novice just had time to say, "The dog..". When silence was lifted he finished the sentence, "..took the roast." By then the roast was toast, the round belly of the dog proved it. The dog innocently wagged his tail in contentment with a dog's grin on the face.

It was tough and painful to sit for hours on your knees in the chapel. As weeks passed on, camel knees appeared (callousness). No more pain nor discomfort while kneeling. The lack of pain in the chapel caused another problem early in the morning: falling asleep instead of meditating. I was so drowsy with sleep every morning. I hooked my arms over the arm rests, slumped over and slept. To make matters worse all windows were kept closed to prevent the stale air from polluting the environment. I asked that the windows be opened but an older monk doused my request. But I was allowed to meditate in a study room all by myself with the windows open at my heart's content. The wholesome fresh air did it to me, I slept like a baby. The trick was not to sleep past the meditation time.

I was in charge of serving the drinks during meals. The faucet water was so bad it had the potential to do you in. I served red wine, Evian water and carbonated water for all meals. No peace for me taking my meals. The constant getting up and serving drinks was a bad idea. I solved my problem by placing fifty bottles of red wine, Evian water and carbonated water on every table. That will do it, it did, but it did not set well with the prior. In the end I even convinced him, he finally agreed as long as there were no visitors in the house (visitors would get the wrong idea about the poor monks displaying hundred of bottle of wine). French People are very content with red wine and a piece of bread for breakfast but not so the Luxemburgers nor the Belges. We need butter. It was granted to me. I argued I needed a lot of bread with butter otherwise I could not function properly. Some days I shared some of my butter with those sitting around me (tongues hanging out a mile). Food really proved to be a problem. I agreed to the vow of poverty but not to starvation. Alternative food sources had to be organized. But you had to stay honest. Any transgression had to be confessed on a weekly basis with all the monks present. This was one of the hardest thing for me. I always tried to phrase my transgression in such a way as to mitigate the punishment. At one of those public confession I said, "I could not resist a Magdalene." Total silence fell over the whole congregation followed by suppressed muttering. The prior sternly fixed his eyes on me and ordered me to repeat what I just said. After I repeated myself, the prior dismissed everybody and told me to see him in his office immediately. The office door was opened so I entered. The prior was sitting behind his desk flanked by two of his counselors, all grimfaced. The prior glasses perched on the tip of his long nose. It reminded me of a vulture. When he talked he kind of hacked his words with the nose. "We need to know all the details. When did it happen?" he uttered. "On Thursday, the day we visited the cathedral of Amiens." We regularly walked to the city in a group. Sometimes some of us wondered off and strolled through the Red District by mistake. "We want to know if there was consummation." Yes, I consumed, it was very good and delicious." Three angry fists hit the desk in unison. "Brother Peacock this is very serious. It looks like you are not monk material at all. Do you have anything more to say for your defense?"

I thought that I did not express myself poetically enough so I said, "I had dinner with a Magdalene and there was consummation afterwards." I insisted on the word consummation because they made such a fuss about it. Their reaction was any than calm nor collected. They shouted by now, "We may have to dismiss you for good from the monastery." I left them and went to my room their last statement still ringing in my ears. I was hungry and pulled my last piece of bread from under the mattress and devoured it. The next day my co-monks ask me repeatedly, "Did you really engaged in sex with a prostitute?" I was horrified, "Where did you get that idea?" "You said it yourself that you could not resist a Magdalene." It turned out that a Magdalene is a prostitute. Now I was surprised. Those monks really thought that I slept with a prostitute. All I did I took a cupcake from the monastery fridge called 'Magdalene' and consumed it with pleasure.

Alternative sources of food had to be found. Days later rats came to my rescue. They were busy chewing fist size holes in the wooden stairs. They were deceived. Do not go to any monastery looking for food unless you are ready to do some starving. The prior summoned the whole congregation to announce that we needed some cats to ward off the rat invasion. We will need a competent cat care taker immediately. As a good Cat-tholic I volunteered on the spot to feed three kittens twice daily. To prevent cat's diarrhea I suggested cooked rice mixed with milk (six months minimum). So I fed the little creatures without forgetting my own stomach. Like magic the rats disappeared. They finally wised up. It was not so much the kittens than the lack of food but I was not going to tell the monks.

There were other food sources I readily tapped into. I saw the garden monk pointing his finger to the left and to the right standing in front of a pear tree. First I thought he was playing ini mini mini mo. In actuality he was counting the ripe pears. Of course we were forbidden to eat between meals or to plug pears from the tree and eat them. I found the solution. Nobody ever told us that we could not eat pears as long as they were hanging on the tree. So I eat the pears while hanging, I ate most of it but the core was still decorating the tree. The garden monk saw it, scratched his head and went his way muttering in his beard. I never was caught and I decided not to confess. Only God knows how they would misunderstand me.

Every day we read the Bible. I really enjoyed it. The lighting was so poor a mouse could not find her way around. Six thirty watts bulbs illuminated the study. Many of us already needed glasses but I was not going to join them. I went on strike instead. No more Bible study under such condition. It worked, six one hundred fifty watts bulbs made their debut. Now plenty of lights to illuminate the truth of the Scriptures. Strike can be good even in a monastery.

When our taming stalled, the prior called for a three week retreat. We were divided into two groups for practical reasons. During retreat nobody was to speak nor make signs except for the sign of the cross. While one group was mute the other group did the daily chores preventing the monastery from chaos. The three weeks past quickly. It gave me tremendous time to converse with God. Helas, I was deemed unfit so I had to join the second group for another three weeks of absolute silence. Your inner conversation goes berserk and there were no cheerleaders to spur you on. Right at that time the bishop of Amiens came to visit the monastery to talk to us about his underwear after he tested our spiritual knowledge. Twelve months had passed, time to profess the vows. The occasion called for a serious examination by the bishop. One of us did not do to well. After many howlers my friend finally gave a correct answer. Ironically the bishop asked him, "My dear do you have many such oases in your knowledge?" "Certainly your Eminence", he replied, "But the camels cannot always find them." He like myself were not permitted to be professed as monks but we all took part in a banquet after the ceremony.

During diner Monseigneur Storm told us about his American tour and how he took New York by storm. In other cities he traveled incognito which caused him sometimes troubles. In a cathedral where he wished to say mass, the sacristan insisted that he wears a slip, a white slip. "No slip no mass," he said. Monseigneur only knew one meaning of slip: underwear, undies. In the end the sacristan brought a slip for Monseigneur. It turned out to be an alleluia, a cassock.

For ministers and priest it is always wise to travel with clean underwear in the suitcase. Father Martin, a Catholic monk, visited his aging mother in Germany. On his return he had to pass through custom of the Vancouver International Airport. The custom official opened his suitcase for a thorough inspection. Father stepped a little to the side quite embarrassed while thinking about his dirty underwear and socks. The custom official smilingly said, "Father we understand, we understand." Glad to have survived the ordeal, Father hurried to the exit to be intercepted by a security guard, flanked by a young beautiful lady. "Father can you check the tag of your suitcase," the guard insisted. Father did. It read, "Dr. Maria…." They exchanged suitcases. The suitcases were identical except for the tags and the content of course. Father turned fire red, ashamed like never before in his life. Now he understood the custom officials who pocked around in 'his' suitcase among the lady's underwear.

The prior posted a sign over the bathtub saying, "An angel is watching you." I added underneath, "What a pig." Six months sentence were added to my novice time. I knew I had to tame myself further. Uneventful months followed except for two incidents that colored this period. Out of the blue every monk became extremely itchy. I really was itchy. In drove the monks assaulted the local doctor's office. Prescriptions were handed out to no much avail. Those prescriptions could have killed the sturdiest monk. I refused any of them. I looked for the cause and found it: fleas and a lot of them. To do the garden work we clothed ourselves with centuries old cassocks. Those cassocks were worn rain or shine. Even full fledged monks get wet under rain and sweaty and stinky in the sun. The fleas proliferated in those clothing and waited on us for a meal. Rashes covered every part of every monk body. Just use your imagination a little bit. Picture a dog scratching himself, then multiply that by forty. The worst was chapel time when every monk kneeled piously till the fleas woke up for breakfast. One monk would scratch himself, then two more and so forth till all forty monks were in action. They say to have a life like a dog without fleas, how about to have a life like a monk without fleas (put on the dog, put on the monk?). I solved the rash problem. Flea bitten, but happy I made my way to the prior to tell him the flea news. I suggested that every monk should wear a dog collar, a flea dog collar the ones you can buy in a pet store. He did not buy into that idea because he said, "It is unbecoming for monks to wear dog collars." I should have gotten a reduced sentence (novice time) but no, instead we burned the old clothing and scrubbed the monastery top to bottom. Years later I experienced first hand how effective flea collars are. Pedro had a dog teaming with fleas. I told him to get a flea collar. A week later I ask him, "How is the dog?" He retorted, "The dog is fine, now I need a flea collar."

That year a fellow monk, who was over the hill, kicked the bucket. He died suddenly. Sombrely we all marched behind his coffin to the cemetery. It was cold, bitter cold. The mood changed drastically on our way back to the monastery. The monks were laughing and had spring in their walk. I did not understand. Why were the monks so happy to have lost a brother monk? I had to ask and was told, "Because of the extreme cold weather the grave could not be dug out. Therefore the late monk was shacked up with a young nun who had passed away a few days earlier. Furthermore he (the late monk) is lying on top of the nun.

Time flowed like a stagnant pond but the end of the noviciate inevitable came. I expected great changes and improvements as a full fledged monk. I left all disappointments behind and settled in Belgium (I was settled and had no say in it). It was a college with about one hundred fifty students, taught and trained by the monks. I became kind of a fifth wheel with all kinds of duties neither being too fulfilling. One great thing, I had more free time to talk to God while roaming the forests. The monastery and school were wedged between two steep mountains. A tiny creek squeezed itself among rocks. The whispering water teamed with trouts and other fish creatures while wild ducks' squawk echoed throughout the valley. Now I was closer to good food sources to supplement the monk's ration. The wild ducks lay their eggs among the pebbles in the creek for me to collect. I found a retired electric hot plate which I installed in the cellar. I could make my one wild tea and boil duck eggs. I also was in charge of the garden and the fruit trees. I decided what to plant and what not to plant. Peas and carrots became my good friends and so did the apples and pears. The monks knew that I was eating on the side (fruits and vegetables) but I assured them that it was for their own good and safety. "I must taste everything before I bring it to you. I take all the risk, I am your cupbearer." They realized that I had a point and a well stocked stomach.

One day I presented to the monks a glass bottle with a very narrow neck with a ripe pear inside. I ask them to meditate how the pear got into the glass bottle. They were at a loss, all those professor monks. In fact it is very easy. You take a tiny pear branch with a tiny pear on it and insert it into the bottle, attach the bottle to the pear tree and let nature take its course. Now the pear grows and grows till it is ripe for consumption.

The dining room table was big and rectangular in shape. As the last comer I was seated at the end. To me that was the head of the table. The prior and his advisers sat in the middle of the table with no overview unless they turned their heads to the left or to the right. During summer break many of the monks went to parishes to give those priests a break too. At times there were only a handful of monks left which could pose a problem. Those monks were mostly elderly monks and they too were seated in the middle of the table. The plates were placed in the middle of the table so the elderly monks could easily serve themselves but I had to get up constantly to get some food for myself. After awhile I had enough. I took the prior's seat and the problem was solved I thought. Apparently you do not do that, you do not put on the monk.

One lazy late fall night, the whole monastery was rocked by an explosion (2 A.M.) All the monks came out of their rooms still groggy with sleep. They put their heads together, "What can this be?" In time I developed a reputation. Suddenly a light went on in their heads. "Brother Peacock," they shouted. At that very moment another explosion, stronger than the first one, shook the building on its foundation. By then I scrambled out of bed annoyed by all the fracas. Heavy hammering on my door indicated that someone was not too happy with me at this hour of the night. Yet another explosion ripped through the night. I rushed to the cellar followed by many very angry voices. One look in the basement gave me the answer: sauerkraut. Sauerkraut was everywhere, floor, ceiling and walls, a real mess. When I made sauerkraut I used urns in the shape of a pear with a very narrowing neck. I cut wood to top the filled urns with cabbage and loaded them with heavy rocks. Through fermentation the rocks are moved upwards but in my case they could not because of the narrowing necks. The power became so great that the urns had to explode. My mistake but it was all worth it.

Some of the novices were sent home for not being real monk material. One of a new crop of novices snapped. He kind of lost his marbles. Sending him home would not have been good monk policy. The priors of a few monasteries put their heads together to find a solution to the dilemma. During some of their debates monk Peacock caught their attention. The priors reasoned, "If brother James (the one who lost his marbles) turns nutty while being among sane monks why don't we put him in the care of the nutty monk Peacock?" All agreed. One late summer day, brother James was transferred to the monastery were I, brother Peacock resided. I gladly took him under my wings. He was tame like a sheep, to me, nothing much was wrong with him. He seemed more normal to me than all the others. Most of the day we spent our time together. Within months he was totally cured and he became an asset to me, helping me greatly to get into monk trouble.

To attract more students, the monastery decided to expand the sports fields particularly a track-and- field. There was but one problem: a massive evergreen tree towering one hundred eighty feet tall. I quickly volunteered to cut it down at no cost. No need to hire a tree cutting firm. All what I had, was a saw to be handled by two. James on one side and I on the other side. In the beginning everything appeared to be going as it should. More than half through the sawing a rather nasty wind came up. It was blowing in the wrong direction (according to me). Since the tree was close to the boundary, it could easily fall on the neighbor's house and crash it. Quick action was of the essence. I ordered James to climb the tree and attach a rope at the one hundred twenty feet level. Willingly he obeyed, proof of his new found sanity. In meantime I hurried to the chapel were all the monks were praying. I whispered to the prior of our ordeal and ask him to bring all the assembled monks to the field. Now I was in charge. I ordered every monk, including the prior, to get hold of the rope and at my command (remember I was in the army) to pull on it as if their lives depended on it. The tree stood his ground, the rope snapped and all the forty monks dressed in their black cassocks like dominos hit the dust. Dusty they were and angry too, possible scientific language was mixed with the dust. I kind of grinned. I am not a revenge full person nevertheless it felt kind of good. I urged everybody to return to the chapel for fervent prayer. We needed a wedge to sway the giant tree to lean away from the house. I found an old ax with a broken handle, that did the trick. James and myself did some more see-sawing. By eight PM the tree came thundering down exactly where we wanted it to fall. We were proud of ourselves, it called for a celebration while all the other monks were praying. I had my own wine cellar just for occasions like this and others. Each time a Congolese or Sudanese missionary returned for vacations, we all celebrated with wine, cake, cookies and smoking. I neither drank wine nor smoke but ate cake and cookies and how I wished to have some grape juice to drink. About ten other monks felt like me but were afraid to do something about it. I ordered from the purchasing monk six of the best grape juice bottles plus other things (the grape juice was double the price of a bottle of wine). Everything I stored in my own wine cellar for freshness and readability if needed. Gladly I shared with the other monks who did not drink alcohol either. They were all delighted but not so the prior. I was interrogated severely about it, "Never in the monastery's history had a single monk his own wine cellar." In the end reason prevailed and I was to keep my own wine cellar (grape juice cellar) thanks to the other monks who saw a common good in it.

From time to time the Provincial Superior, the authority over all the Belgian and Luxemburger monasteries, came for a visit to check the finances and the orderly running of the monastery. That day I was asked to replace James in the sacristy (the prior did not want to take chances with James). I prepared everything for the mass of the Provincial (kind of an honor). All went well, the Provincial consecrated the bread and the wine and then he took part of it. Suddenly he startled, then spat! The prior went to him then ran to me. With the prior in tow I ran to the sacristy to inspect the wine bottle I had used for the mass. Close scrutiny revealed that someone had poured liquid soap in a wine bottle the one I had used for the preparation of the mass. I got an earful from the prior while the Provincial was blowing bubbles at the altar. Incidents like this and many others did not further my reputation as a monk. Somehow the tide turned against me. I acquired a past without a future as a monk.

A very bad toothache triggered a turning point. Dental attention was urgently needed. Sitting in the dental chair did not indicated that something awfully was wrong. Hours later when the freezing subsided, more terrible toothaches appeared. To my horror a perfectly healthy tooth was missing. The tooth with the cavity was still there and hurting badly. I went back to the dentist who was very apologetic and ashamed. He had followed the prior advice, "Pull the tooth." They did not believe me that I really had a toothache. They thought this was just another trick of me I was pulling on them. I also noticed that after eating I felt sick. I confronted the prior and told him that we were drugged. First he denied everything categorically but when I insisted that I overheard him talking about drugs to one of his advisors he quickly said, "Not anymore, not anymore." That was a lie. From then on the monks did everything to get me leave the monastery. I switched into survival mode. During adoration in the chapel I was ordered to clean the chimney, the septic tank or any other dirty task.

Months past, I enjoyed a great time with God during those trying times. The monks became desperate and decided to kick me out, but I smelled the rat. I wrote to my family that soon I would be thrown out of the monastery and that they could expect me soon. My family lived in Canada. I knew that my mail was intercepted and the prior was reading it. Here I had a great opportunity to manipulate the prior in the way I wrote my letters. He fell for it. It also gave them the idea to send me to Canada, to join the monks there which would take care of the problem (meaning me). It gave me new hope even though I was never permitted to profess the perpetual vows. The question why did they use drugs in the food and why did they wanted to get rid of me so badly, still haunt me today.

A year ago God showed me a vision about a monk on his death bed begging me for forgiveness. He was the one I thought was my friend.

I was shipped to Canada as an undesirable. I felt like a criminal, rejected by his own. With great eagerness I boarded the ship and sought out my cabin. To my surprise my cabin was already occupied by a very angry Dutch man. He told me to take a hike and get lost. I took his advice, no use to hassle with a guy three times your size. The officer on duty assigned another cabin to me, very roomy and with a bull's eye. I might as well sail in style. The next night we accosted another port to take on more passengers. At 1 AM a heavy knock at my door jolted me out of my sleep. An angry voice insisted that this was his cabin, that I opened the door immediately and that I vacate the cabin on the spot. I knew the feeling, I just chuckled under the blankets and went back to sleep.

I kept in the centre of the ship as much as possible because there is less upheaval from the waves just to keep my stomach in sink. At meals we were asked in what languages we were fluent, and then were given menus in a total foreign language to us. With stomachs already on edge the weird dishes we ordered made us feed the fish over the railing. The dining rooms were mostly empty by the end of three weeks. I understand now why sailors like to drink alcohol. When drank it will counteract the heaving of the ship, so they walk straight. Our sailing came to an end in Montreal. I spend a couple of weeks with my family then Pedro drove me to the monastery in Chateauguay. It was a college located in a rural setting, quite promising. However the next day I was transferred to a monastery in Montreal where the monks seminarians dwelt. Later I learned that a letter from Europe prompted the change. Somehow I got the impression that everybody thought that I was a hopeless nut case. There were so many drugs in the food that I almost became blind and acted irrationally. The day I suggested to fertilize the garden with ice melting salt, my case was sealed. The cook went on holiday and I replaced him. I was a trained electrician not a cook. The closest to wiring were the spaghettis. I cooked a lot of them, they mostly clamped together and sometimes they fell in the sink. The seminarians had no choice but to eat whatever I prepared for them (one hour lunch break). I cooked what I liked with plenty of raw vegetables. I gained weight, never heard of in the monastery but the other monks lost weight not an uncommon thing. As the cook I had some control over the drug problem.

During summer vacations most of the seminarians went home and some of the monk priests went to parishes to give the parish priests a reprieve for a few weeks. The prior, a Dutch, went to Holland. One senior monk and adviser to him replaced him while he was in Holland. I felt this was the right time to confront and grill him about the mixing of harm full drugs in the food. My position was clear: as long as he would admit it and promised to stop the non-sense I would stay in the monastery. He did not say anything but shook like an aspen leaf. He was not going to compromise himself nor the prior. Quickly I packed my bags, called Pedro to pick me up. Nobody prevented me from leaving the monastery, if they had I would have punched them out cold. My monk life came to an end. A few more weeks and my vows expired too. The prior with one of his adviser showed up after two weeks. He had a document he wanted me to sign. The Father General in Rome had accepted my resignation. They urged me to sign which I did. Then they urged me to sign a second copy they said. The second copy was all covered by the first copy except for the signature line. I signed without hesitation. All this took place near the dung heap. A few weeks later I received a copy of what I had signed: a copy of my resignation and to my great surprise I document bearing my signature that I could never sue them for any wrong doing on their part. Those bastards there was no truth in them, they just tricked me. It never crossed my mind to sue them in the first place. I was so relieved not being a monk anymore and found it totally useless to complain to any of those goons. But I complained to the Pope: Paul the Sixth and gave him a letter full of human rights violations, deceitfulness and harmful drugs disguised in the daily meals. The monastic life ought to create an environment where all the monks can mature and become healthy in every aspect of their human nature: spirit, mind and body. It should not be a place where anyone is alienated and withers. If that is the case, that person should shake off the dust and leave in a hurry. It is not of God but of the evil one. The Pope wrote me back and apologized sort of. He also send me fifty dollars, a gold medal of his and the promise that he would pray for me. It is the custom to pray every Sunday in every Catholic Church for the intentions of the Pope. That means at one time 1.2 billion people prayed for me. The people around me think I really needed it.

New Found Freedom

A new chapter in my life took roots. No time to waste. Immediately I started working on Pedro's vegetable farm (350 acres). In Quebec you have six months good weather for farming and six months winter (or almost for gaining weight). Transition times are kept to a minimum by nature (three weeks). It was hard work, fifteen hours daily six days a week. A lot of pulling weeds while crawling on your knees (the camel knees from the monastery came handy), not the most inspiring work one can think of. Pedro paid me one dollar per hour. The going rate was sixty cents. At the time the price of a crate for twenty four head lettuce was greater than the lettuce itself. When that happened we plowed the lettuce fields under. I was grieved seeing the hunger in the world and here we were destroying good food. On Sundays we moved to the city where our parents owned a nice brick house. Our father also worked on the farm. Nobody could keep pace with him. Other workers refused to work with him for that reason.

Sunday was the only day of rest, but by five PM we already returned to the farm to get a good start on Monday morning. Sundays we went to a Catholic Church in the small town we lived. It was also the only day for me to look out for girls. By then I was determined to find a suitable girl to get married. My first attempt to make friends was a failure. There was this very beautiful girl who drove to church every Sunday. I thought asking her for a ride home would be perfect to make contact with her. The words I used in French were out of place to say the least. "Can you please kidnap me." I did not get any further. She pressed the gas pedal and gone she was for good. I heard her muttering, "What a weirdo." In that church I met another pretty young girl. She was a college student very pleasant to be with. I gave her a nice book about motherhood. She really liked it. We arranged for a date, our first date. When I knocked at the door her mother informed me that her daughter had to finish her studies first before any dating. May be the motherhood book had something to do with it. Possibly my occupation as a farm worker had something to do with it too. Farm workers are not sought after for marriage. I scored my failure number two.

I love books, books about human nature. Whenever I had an opportunity I visited the local bookstore. There I met the manager, a very lovely young girl (at that age most young girls are lovely). Before I could arrange for a date I was told by her staff that she was traveling across Europe. I could wait. I kept her phone number in a safe place and tried to contact her from time to time. She was still traveling. Months later I finally got hold of her. We agreed for a date in her apartment(kind of a blind date). When I laid eyes on her, I was shocked: she was big, very big. Out of courtesy I did not asked how she got pregnant (I knew anyhow). I enjoyed her cooking and left disappointed: failure number three.

In the winter I would go to church on weekdays as well. The parish priest was very kind to arrange a job interview with a church member who had an electrical company (twenty five workers). Very happy, I started with $1,65 hourly rate. Most of the twenty five workers were working in a factory where laminates were manufactured. Outdoor temperatures were well below zero but indoor, especially under the ceiling, the temperatures made you sweat. They added a major section to the factory which provided work for the electricians for months. Most of construction came to a standstill during the winter with the very low temperatures and heaps of snow. At first, everybody welcomed me and they were all helpful and friendly. Within one week all that changed. I noticed most of them came one hour late and left one hour early. I always came in time and left after a full eight hour shift. While I was waiting for the others to arrive I put law and order into the material. I sorted bolts and nuts and so forth every thing nice and neat. To my horror some workers messed everything up again on purpose just to annoy me.

We had to drink a lot because of the extreme heat in the factory. The foreman asked me if I would like to buy a coke, he would get it for me. When I got the coke it was hot, the foreman boiled it for me. I took everything in stride at least for the time being. I was so glad to have a job as electrician, I work like a horse. That was a mistake. Another time the foreman told me to work on electrical equipment under the ceiling. I was sweating profusely, while handling the wires he turned the power on to get me jolted. I constantly tested for power otherwise it would have killed me. Three weeks into the job I was called to the office. The boss told me, "Peacock you are fired, you work too much. All the workers told me either Peacock goes or we go. Therefore I have to let you go."

I started to have doubts about Canada. The monks let me down, the girls let me down and the workers let me down. In Luxembourg my boss increased my wages by one third and here I am fired. The future looked bleak, very bleak. Then the temperature let me down too. I had it. Forty below zero, that spelled an unwelcoming land, an unforgiving land. On the spot I decided to leave, but where to? A quick look at the Canada map solved the problem: Vancouver British Columbia. Within three days I was on my way never to return. My parents and brothers welcomed my departure for a better future. They promised me to follow as soon as I would get a job and become self sufficient. "Do not ask for financial support; if you do we will not come to B.C..

I traveled light with only one suitcase. My brother-in-law from Australia travelled even lighter. When he arrived at the Vancouver airport the officials called him and apologized for having lost his luggage. "Not to worry about it," he said, "I have no suitcase only a lunchbox." The lunchbox contained a loaf of bread and underwear. Whatever he needed he would buy and leave everything behind when he left. He wanted to enjoy travel without becoming a pack mule.

I was eager to see Canada. For hours I starred into the endless landscapes of middle and western provinces. There was nothing to see except snow covered prairies and farmland. The other train passengers would tip their heads while looking in my direction. They thought that I was nuts, they knew that there was nothing to see. That changed drastically when we entered the Rocky Mountains. Finally I got rewarded with an exciting mountain scape.

In Vancouver I rented one room in a large old house from a Dutch lady. Repeated trips to the local manpower centre yielded no job. I did not speak English. Other renters in the same house suggested that I should apply for welfare. Only then, they said, would I get a job. Get rid of all your money first, otherwise you do not qualify. I needed about seven hundred dollars a month for rent, food and friends. I took my friends out for diner from time to time. Since I had no work I spend most of my time on the beach, sun tanning and plain enjoying the sea. I took the advice from my friends and got rid of all my money except $ 35.00. I bought a Volkswagen Beetle. I had a driver license, but I had never driven a car in my life. The sales person took me on the road so that I might get accustomed to the new car. I was driving. His hair spiked immediately. Horrified he ordered me to return to the dealership. "You must get insurance right now," he stuttered. He could not comprehend that I purchased the car with cash but had no money for insurance. Next I drove the car to a parking lot at the beach and exercised the car as good as I could. Then I drove home and parked the car in front of the house and left it there. I had no money to drive it anymore. Gas was too expensive (thirty cents per gallon).

I walked on foot to the welfare centre. Ten days ago they had promised me a check. Things were looking up. By then I could no longer pay for rent, the welfare check would take care of that too. The clerk became very animated by the sound of my name. He booted me out of the office. "You have a brand new car, you do not qualify for any check." Now I had to face the landlady. She was very kind and offered me a month free rent. "By the way, she said, "There is a nice car parked in front of the house do you have any idea to whom it may belong?" "It is mine," I stammered. Nevertheless she upheld her offer. I could not ask my family to help me out, they would not join me if I needed their help. I targeted the Salvation Army for a sandwich voucher. At least I would not go hungry. With the voucher in my pocket I walked to East Hastings where I could redeem the voucher. By the time I arrived, the place was closed. God had another plan. If he could send a raven to feed the prophet he could send me help too.

An American, called Jim, moved in next to my room. He fled to Canada to evade being drafted to the Vietnam war. His father send him money on a monthly basis to keep him alive and well. Jim volunteered to support me with a weekly five dollars allowance. What a blessing, the Vietnam War proofed to be good after all. Jim also took me along to his many girlfriends. Both of us were delighted in all the food those girls dished up for us.

Weeks later I received a call from the manpower centre. I was asked to go for a job interview in one of the suburbs of Vancouver. I took my Beetle along with me because no bus would go to that location. "The job is yours under one condition: you must have a car or we cannot hire you," I was told. Guess what, I had a car.

One of the co-workers was worried, because I did not have car insurance. He had nightmares about it. Just to please him I bought insurance. It was not too early. Three weeks later on my way to work someone drove through the red light in an intersection thinking my green car was the green light. He just plowed into me. In turn my car hit two other cars parked by the side of the road. Both car owners sued me for as much as they could. Thanks to my insurance they were taken care off. My green Beetle was a write-off. I got a new Beetle, a red one, so no one would think I was the green light. With additional money from the claim, I bought appliances and dining room furniture.

Three weeks on the job I got a substantial raise. Some of the workers were not too happy about that. They thought six weeks would be better. I could not more disagree with them.

One of the workers had the same first name as one of the bosses. He was told, "From now on your first name is Ludwig, your pay cheque will also bear your new name: Ludwig." We all knew him as Ludwig. I made some good friends in that place but some were not too keen about me.

The leadership of the company was intrigued by me. We made control panels for the forest industry and other manufacturers. A typical console required about thirty hours of intense labour. I did them in about twenty hours. The extra ten hours were credited to a friend of the boss. At the beginning I had no clue how the rabbit was running but when I found out I resented it. It was also part of the reason that I quit that job two years later.

We were part of a labour union. As such we routinely went on strike and some of us were laid off. I was ask if I would learn nameplate engraving then I would not be laid off. Of course I agreed, I needed money badly. I also worked nightshift during my holidays. The engraving machine was any but sophisticated, most of the measurement were by eyesight only. It was a nerve wrecking task. Today those machines are all computerized. You made one little mistake just before you finished an eight hour nameplate and you had to start all over again. In time I went back to console wiring again. But first I had to train a young girl in engraving. In the corner of the engraving room stood a table saw to cut the plastics for engraving but it also was used to cut asbestos sheets by other workers. When the girl moved in, the table saw was moved out because of health concerns. Six months later the girl was assigned a new task and I went back to engraving. The saw was also moved back to that room. That move broke the camel's back. I just quit the job all together. Two years were enough to claim credit for work experience so that I could write the exam for Canadian electrical journeyman class C and B.

While still working, my two brothers, Fred and Lion, drove to British Columbia to join me. We rented a basement apartment. The landlady was quiet concerned about three young fellows making a lot a noise. The noise makers were the renters from upstairs. A cabdriver who drank heavily with his wife. Often he would chase his teenage son out the front door and back in through the back door at night. She was following him to prevent him from harming their son.

Our electrical bill went sky high. I investigated. The lady upstairs did laundry for other people. Our hot water tank was interconnected with her water tank. The double garage was rented to yet another person. That person charged many car batteries day and night. The electricity came from our meter. I refused to pay two months rent to make up for it. The landlady, flanked by a B.C.Hydro official and a city inspector, pleaded with me to pay the two months rent. I did not, but decided to move to another place instead. In meantime I earnestly looked for a place of my own. A two acre pine treed lot with a house on it caught my attention. Asking price was only six thousand dollars, a real steal. Next to it the same size of a lot without a house was listed for eight thousand dollars. I made a hundred dollar down payment to the real estate agent and pointed out to him the discrepancy with the next door lot. That was a mistake. The agent bought it and returned the hundred dollars to me.

I looked for another property closer to Vancouver. That property was about three acres but no house nor trees on it. I offered two third of the asking price in cash, cash I did not have. I went to the bank for a loan, expecting to get it. The bank refused to give me anything. Apparently if you do not have anything they do not give you anything. The neighbor of the property also made an offer. He paid full asking price. There were two lots to be had. The owners were very eager to sell, so far they did not have any prospecting buyers for two years. Because I was the first one to make them an offer they told me I could made them another offer. I offered them the full asking price but they had to lend me the money for one year, then I promised to pay them off plus interest. They agreed. Here I was, I just quit my job, I had no money (very little) and I bought this property.

The place I rented was a duplex. The rent was cheap, one hundred seventy five dollars a months. The problem was, it was for sale which I did not know. Each time the landlord showed the place to a prospecting buyer I retained twenty dollars. Now I encouraged him to come more often. The owner did not go for it, he went to court instead. The judge pronounced his verdict, "Mr. Peacock you are right but you have to pay your rent in full." I made arrangement with the landlord so that I could stay in his place. After that he only showed the house to one buyer who bought the duplex. The new owner was a real pain in the neck.

The telephone company was very slow in providing a telephone for me. Cell phones were not yet invented. At times I would visit their local office and asked if I could make a call. They aloud me to do so, obviously they did not get the message. That summer it was very hot and no rain for six months, the perfect time for me to call my parents. I made the long distance call, I had plenty of coins to feed the public phone. Every few minutes the operator reminded me to add more coins. In the heat of the conversation I forgot to insert more coins and so did the operator. An hour later the operator ordered me to insert thirty dollars of coins. By now the phone refused any more money. I told the operator my good luck. "Hang up and we will bill your telephone (which I did not have)." Ten people were waiting impatiently for their turn to make a call. They saw my facial expression from angry to laughing then angry again. "This man is insane let us get him out of the phone booth," they shouted in unison. One last thing the operator did for me: she released all the coins for me to pocket them. Now the ten people were even more convinced that they were dealing with a lunatic. The loot amounted to over sixty dollars. Days later a letter from the company urged me to pay thirty dollars but there was one big problem: they cannot invoice you unless you have a phone from them. I made a deal with the manager: install my phone and I will pay the thirty dollar. I never mentioned the windfall. The next day I got my phone installed, now is that service or not?

Within a week my mother joined us in Vancouver. As soon as she stepped on the tarmac the sky opened and poured out rain for the next six months just to make up for the six months of gorgeous weather prior to that.

We build our house and with that we got neighbors. In all we build three houses. Unfortunately we did it all wrong. The first house you should build for your enemy, the second for your friend and the third for yourself. We did it the other way around.

My left neighbor was a Dutch horse farmer. He was very good in horse trading.

The first time I met him, he sternly pointed out the boundary between us two. I let him believe that what he thought was the truth. Right away I noticed that he was totally wrong. My property instantly gained ten feet in width by seven hundred sixty feet in length. I could live with that. I planted pine trees in that section. By now they are eighty feet tall. Other neighbors told me, "Do not work for him, you will wind up paying him instead of he paying you." I accepted the warning.

We (Fred and I) wired his newly build barn. It was our first job as electrical contractors. While working for him we got to know him too. He sold the tamest horse (according to him) to a lady. The next day she came crying, "Your tame horse threw me off and then took off, what do I do now?" He rented out horses all day long especially on weekends. Some sued him for broken bones but he kept changing his business name to avoid being dragged to court. To me he was Van Donkey (he had a donkey too). He paid us three thousand dollars but left the balance of three hundred dollars unpaid. I removed some of the new light fixtures we just installed for payment and left it at that. A year later he asked me, "Do I owe you anything? "Nope, I answered. He wanted more work done. This time he had to pay us in full before we even started to work.

For many years he tried to get his farmland taken out of the land reserve and rezoned for commercial use but to no avail. I provided him with color photos from previous flooding. Thanks to those photos the city counselors approved his application. The deal was that he also would get my land out of the land reserve, but he did not plead my case. His land use changed from agricultural to commercial. By the stroke of a pen the value soared to over a million dollars. The change came with some obligations. The land had to be surveyed and a fence had to be erected between me and him. "As a good neighbor," he told me, "you must pay for half of the surveying costs and half of the fence costs." I gently responded, "Fly a kite." The survey finally proofed to him where the real boundary between him and me was. It made him spite and holler in scientific language. It got so bad he almost had to be admitted to the mental institution. Recently I found out that he had cancer. I prayed for him for God to intervene in his life. He sold the property for a very good price. The property lies unused ever since.

We also had a very pleasant neighbor: a Japanese retired couple. He did not understand any English. I gesticulate while saying all kind of nonsense to him. He responded by wheeling a wheelbarrow full of fruits and vegetables to my place. Even though he was retired he gardened himself silly. He breathed, lived, worked and ate in a one acre garden, a real jewel. The sweetness of his watermelons testified to that. One day a heavy wind storm tumbled one of my evergreen trees (one hundred twenty feet tall). He left town for a few days. Time enough to hire a crane and erect the tree. Guy wires and nylon ropes kept it from falling over again. When my neighbor returned he was puzzled to the extreme. He was running up and down in his garden, scratching himself behind the ears. He could not make sense of the standing up tree.

A fox invaded my chicken coop and scared the hell out of the chicken as well as of the rooster. That was the last I heard from my flock. The next day my neighbor's barn emitted hen and rooster speech. Was it a coincidence or what, I left it at that. Another time he came to me while I was tending my goats. He made signs and gestures pointing to one of my goats and to his mouth. Clearly he intended to eat that goat. I had to talk to him with an interpreter. This was serious business. A time was set for the weekend, him providing the interpreter.

Saturday afternoon I visited him. A large table full of the most delicious food greeted me. I asked the interpreter, "Who are the guests?" "You," he replied. For the next three hours I gorged myself with the most exotic foods I ever had tasted.

Finally I put the question to him, "Why do you want to eat my goat?" He looked surprised, then both the neighbor and the interpreter burst into laughter. "No, no your goat ate his corn," chuckled the interpreter. Now I laughed too. Years later he sold his property with great regret to leave his garden behind. He called me one more time. By then he spoke some English. He offered me his chicken including a rooster with a sack of chickenfeed. When I lay eyes on his chicken I realized they were my chicken and my rooster. The fox had scared them to his barn and he accepted gladly the windfall of chicken. I could not tell him, it would have hurt him.

My right neighbor changed every few years. Once we had a young couple who liked to party a lot. The husband liked to repair cars, mostly sheet metal work. His workshop was just in front of our bedroom window. The real problem was that he would get active after midnight to five in the morning. Hammering the dents out of accidented automobiles does not further your sleep. After awhile we could not take it anymore. The police was called to dampen his nightly enthusiasm. Two hours later he restarted again. I threatened to install a getto blaster on top of my roof to teach him a lesson in noise pollution. Before I even could buy a blaster he did it the next night. That killed the friendly atmosphere between us for good.

Some of my trees were already on a leash which the neighbor thought was unsafe for their children. The neighbor's wife called the city official. He instructed me to cut all my trees for safety concern. I requested that their trees should be cut first, otherwise no go. All the trees are still standing to this very day.

The neighbor's house sits just opposite an intersection. With eighteen hundred trucks rumbling through the intersection a night made their house hopping literally. They got their own medicine in noise pollution. She decided to sell the house. She fought hard to get the trucks stopped with any means possible. She came to me waving an olive branch. "We can only win if we fight together," she said. I agreed even though I had no problem. I built my house two hundred feet from the road so that road traffic would not bother me at all. The news papers reported was called for an interview. A detailed report appeared in the local paper telling about our plight with a picture of her and me. The photographer who took the picture constantly reminded me to look mean. The next day she showed me the article. "You have not a single mean bone in your face and I look like I just murdered someone (that's the way you looked like). Some of my friends also saw the picture thinking that my neighbor was my wife. "We feel sorry for you." "Do not feel sorry for me because she is my neighbor and not my wife," I said. After degrading her property for more than a year she sold it at a loss of more than one hundred thousand dollars. What do you expect if you continually tell the world how bad the location is.

To have good neighbors start with you. Be a good neighbor and most likely you will have good neighbors. If your neighbor has the same first and last name as yourself that may cause some confusion. I know of such a case. Here is this guy, called Al, Al Turnbull, who moved to a suburb of Vancouver. The first day he went to greet his new neighbor. "My name is Al, Al Turnbull nice to meet you, I am your new neighbor." As a reply he heard, "My name is Al Turnbull nice to meet you too." "No, no my name is Al Turnbull not yours," they both uttered perplexed. In the end both realized that they had the same name, first and last and totally unrelated. For the mail man it was not a laughing matter but rather a nightmare. He often delivered the mail to the wrong Turnbull. Time went by peacefully until one of the Turnbulls took in a boisterous renter, a young fellow who liked to party. At one time it got so noisy that Al Turnbull called the police to put a damper on the party animal. The police officer asked Al's name first and last and then the neighbor's name, first and last. The officer became so upset thinking the caller was pulling his leg. In desperation he asked, "Is this a joke?" "Oh no, it is a complaint." In the end one of the Turnbulls turned around and moved to Vancouver Island. The other Turnbull switched to Shaw for his phone and e-mail needs. Telus gave the other Turnbull the e-mail address of the first Turnbull. All the first Turbull's e-mails went now to the Vancouver Island Turnbull: a total fiasco. God has a great sense of humor. He allows, and I think He engineers irritating neighbors to give you an opportunity to tame yourself. Thank Him for it, it is for your own good.

Delivering companies can be a real pain. You expect a parcel and it seems it never comes. We were expecting software (a hard disk not soft at all) from the U.S.A. I drove out that day, standing in my driveway waiting for the traffic to clear so I could proceed. I saw a van pulling out from my neighbor's place. My first reaction was, "Here comes my hard software." He, the driver of the van, past my place. In desperation I blew the horn to make him aware. He took off like a bullet. I followed him in hot pursuit. He turned the corner, drove to the side and parked. I stopped behind him and walked up to the driver. "Sir do you have a parcel for Quest, my address is so and so." "Oh, he said, here it is." He just wrote on the parcel in very big letters: no such address.

Each time I expected a delivery from the same company it became a nightmare. We were told by IBM that a laptop was on its way. That Friday evening I found a yellow slip attached to the mailbox warning me of the first attempt to deliver the laptop. I phoned the company and requested that they tell the delivery man to ring the bell (he did not ring the bell on Friday). The following Monday I stayed home just to take the delivery. By ten I checked the mailbox and there was the second delivery slip. I phoned the company again to be told that it takes forty eight hours to tell the delivery man to ring the bell and if you want to pick it up yourself it takes another forty eight before you can do so. I begged them to make another delivery. This time I would be ready. I placed a large sign on the mail box near the gate. The sign said, "Please ring the bell." The same day the delivery man came back and rang the bell. Nothing happened, not a pip of a sound because at that very moment we experienced a power failure. The next day a very grouchy man rang the bell and the parcel was finally delivered .

Firemen are special people, when everybody runs for safety they run in the fire. At times we had little or no work which prompted us to build a house. Our intention was to sell it afterwards. It took us five years to build. Building a house always comes with problems. The lot we were building on was very stumpy. All those stumps were piled up (twenty feet high). They were ready to be burned. Fred and Lion thought a truck load of old tires might be an excellent idea to get the fire started. While they were gone to fetch the tires I waited impatiently. Armed with a fire permit (for a very small heap) I lit a match to start the burning process. To my surprise it lit and in minutes shot over one hundred feet in the air. The whole neighborhood went berserk and called the fire department. I was kind of apprehensive but when the firemen arrived I was relieved, nothing could go wrong now. The fire chief asked for the permit, tore it up and told his crew to douse the flames. My two brothers arrived with the old tires. I objected to the dousing but to no avail. My reasoning was to let the stumps burn under the supervision of the firemen. In the end we had to wait till winter, relocate the stumps in a tiny heap and then burn them. It was a very time consuming under taking.

Pouring concrete on a very hot day may never be a good idea unless you want to lose weight in a hurry. We were exposed pebble concreting all the sidewalks and the driveway on such a very hot day. The concrete truck driver was very impatient. He allowed us only one hour to do everything then he left and we jumped into action with steel brushes for the final finish. Time was against us, joined by the heat of the day. We labored like madmen till late in the evening. Combined we lost over twenty pounds, we looked like shadows of ourselves. Those were valuable lessons learned the hard way. Science progresses by building on previous knowledge but in child development and marriage one starts from scratch, always. There is one exception to the rule: teenagers know everything, so hire them.

What is a Good Church?

Every husband and or father is responsible to bring his spouse and his children to a good church, a Christian church. That begs the question: What is a good church? A good church is a church with a sign over its entrance saying, "Enter at your own risk!" You will be pre-warned about the good and possibly about the bad. You may enter a sinner and leave a righteous person: a believer, you may enter sick and possibly dying and you may leave totally healed and alive. You may enter financially poor and leave rich, you may enter aimlessly and leave with a purpose, knowing when and were to go. You may enter not knowing about God and not knowing God and you leave knowing about God and knowing God. You may enter hating God and men and leaving loving God and men. A church like that is not only a good church but a perfect church as well. Some preachers say, "There is no perfect church." They are wrong, because nothing is impossible with God. Perfect churches are on God's agenda. Recently I attended a perfect church service. While the preacher preached many were healed in their spirits, other in their bodies and others in their minds. At the end a Muslim lady came out, she asked to become a Christian. Now that is a perfect church service. If we only believed, it would happen all the time. What is the difference between Christian churches and between the different Christian denominations? The differences are their misinterpretations of the Scriptures. All Christian Churches have the same God: God the Father, God the Son and God the Holy Spirit. God deals and interact with His people the same way regardless of their church affiliation. Doctrine is also the same. A true Christian Church's

doctrine is based on Scriptures especially the New Testament, written by the first Roman Catholics. Therefore all denominations are offshoots of the original, early Church: the Roman Catholic Church. If a church does not base their doctrine on the Scripture then that church qualifies as a cult.

And then there are the grace channels. Every Christian church has the grace channels. The Catholic Church says that they have seven grace channels. The Non-Catholics have even more, I counted nine. Of course God is not limited to any numbers. He can dispense His grace in a way and manner He chooses. Some call the grace channels: the sacraments. Let us put numbers on those items:

> Same God fifty per cent
> Scriptures thirty per cent
> Grace channels ten per cent

That gives us a total of ninety per cent. The remaining ten per cent count for the individual calling of a particular church. Churches have different ordinances for how they conduct their services, how their churches are structured, what garment they wear etc. God loves diversity and individuality. All together we make up His body. A foot is different from a hand. Diversity is God willed. It is not healthy to poke fun at any denomination. I have never seen a church prosper that poked fun at the Catholic Church for instance.

Unity among all Christian Churches is possible. It depends on each and every Christian: unity of purpose, unity of doctrine, unity of love in loving God and mankind.

Twenty years ago I looked all over Canada and the U.S.A. to find a church where people entered disabled and left healed. Then one day a German couple told me of such a local church. At that time I was selling by the road side an old Volvo. The couple was interested in buying it. That was the reason we met.

The lady was praying in tongues, on and off with the intention to get the price lowered. I admit it was stiff, the price that is. After a lot of haggling and praying in tongues (lashing in the spirit) it was decided that her husband would take the car to a dealership to get it assessed for possible short comings. As a Catholic and a former Catholic monk, I was not going to leave the local Catholic Church and go to a non-denominational church unless God would tell me so. I made a deal with God. If I must go to their church then this couple must buy the car and pay full asking price. I tried to make it difficult for God. The man took the car to a

Volvo dealership for evaluation. Hours later he returned with two pages of deficiencies. Triumphant he waved it in my face. He also had checked the local newspaper for used car similar to the one I was selling. He wrote me a cheque of two thousand dollars. My reply was, "Since you know exactly what's wrong with the car, this particular car is worth four thousand dollars and not a penny less. He wrote another cheque, this time for four thousand dollars. I was stunt. God held His part of the deal now I had to become a member of 'That Church'. Four thousand dollars were a lot for that couple. They were not poor. They drove a Mercedes Benz to pick up the Volvo. They were not rich either, they tethered the passenger door with a rope strung across their laps at the belly button height. Whoever got out first from the car just untied the rope from the doors. They did it to prevent the door from flinging open while driving.

For the first month I still would attend the Catholic Church in the morning and go to the non-denominational church in the evening. In time I became so unhappy that I quit the Catholic church altogether. The services at the non-denominational church were totally unorthodox, very entertaining sprinkled with people being healed. The things I was looking for.

For the next fifteen years I attended that same church. There was a Wednesday service from six to nine, a Sunday morning service from nine to one or two P.M. and an evening service from five to eleven. Sometimes the last service went to one A.M. into Monday morning. Right from the start I became an usher and for the last ten years the head usher. I never checked my watch, there was no need for it. Time just flew by. You never knew what would happen. Never any bulletin was followed, just open ended service, anything could happen and anything was possible. The way the services were conducted was strictly enforced, the task of the ushers. At one time two opposite gang leaders found their way to the church. Both became Christians, one was killed execution style three months later. Others were sought by the police. They too became Christians and changed their life. It was a good church. A Mafia man came to a Sunday evening service. God showed the pastor that he had a bullet lodged in his lungs. Nobody knew about it except the man himself. When the pastor told him about it, he too became a Christian. Many people were given advice from God through a word of knowledge which changed their lives for the better. The preaching of the pastor was not always sound doctrine but most of the people did not noticed. For me that was a different story. When you are in every service you detect discrepancies. God prevented me from going public so I zipped my mouth. God was more concerned about people being born of Him. The church was only five minutes by car from where I lived. I only missed five services in fifteen years. I attended all three services in the week. Pastor Harry would often go to crusades and minister all over the world. He would take the so called catchers with him. They were strong men, some were bodybuilders. The thing was when pastor Harry prayed for people and laid hands on them, they would fall to the floor under the power of God. The same phenomenon as Paul was slain while riding a horse. Also when Jesus was arrested in the Garden of Gethsemane those who intended to arrest Him fell to the ground. One time in particular there was no catcher to help a visiting preacher. As the head usher I volunteered and ask a fellow usher to help as well. Since he was tall and I was short we agreed that he would catch the men and I would catch the ladies. Generally speaking ladies are lighter than men with some exception. If a three hundred pound lady is about to fall on the floor and you are the one to catch her and place her gently on the floor your work is cut out for you. I devised a very fool proof method because I was not taking any chances to be squashed by such a lady. In the past some catchers just caught the ladies' sweaters. Those ladies did not wear a bra. The ladies fell on the floor with the catchers holding their sweaters exposing their breasts. Things like that were not going to happen to me. The strong catchers used their hands in the back of the people and gently laid them to the ground. I used my arms to catch. From behind, with outstretched arms I let them fall towards me, my arms hooking unto their arms. When they started to fall I also brought my hands towards that person. Even a heavy duty lady you will be able to handle and gently lay her to the ground. Everything went well, at least that's what I thought. This went on for awhile. Suddenly the preacher shouted, "let's have fun together." Only then did I realized what I was doing. With the ladies and girls who fell I did well but those who did not fall and stumble a little bit I still brought my arms under their arms. I also brought my hands towards me meaning towards them and their breasts. In fact I was cupping their breasts, instinctively squeezing them too. All this happened in full view of about two to three hundred people in the church. Half through the service the ladies and girls who came forward for prayer outnumbered the men three to one. I also noticed the women were a lot happier than the men. I was quite busy you could say. By the end the preacher insisted that he prayed for me. I thought it can only help. After the service the ladies and girls came to me and commanded me for the good work I had done. They were looking forward for the next day for a repeat performance on my part. I really felt good. Risbo, the fellow who caught with me warned me, "The men are outraged, especially the leaders who's wives you caught. They say you did not do it right." They will get you tomorrow, so be pre-warned. I replied, "I did not catch any of them how can they say I did not do it right. The girls and ladies told me that I did an excellent job. I believe them." What a disappointment for the girls and ladies the next day. I had to leave early in the service. Later I also used this incident as a good example how not to do it.

In time the atmosphere changed in the church. Some people were asked to spy on people. Some left the church for good. They did not wanted to have anything to do with that. Pastor Harry had surrounded himself with stupid people and some wise people. He did not listen to the wise ones but to the stupid ones. Drugs were introduced to control the members. Drugs were baked into cookies, cakes, mixed into other foods and drinks as well. Pastor Gate became the leader of the spy ministry and also the prime person who decided who would get what drug. They seemed to have everything under control. Hardly anyone knew what was going on. At a Christmas party the food was dispensed by volunteers with the secretary given out the gravy. She had two gravy pots, one normal and one with drugs in it. She had instructions who to give gravy with drugs. I got gravy with drugs. The next morning she phoned me repenting of what she had done. It was too late. Many became ill and some became suicidal. They did not know what was happening to them. One guy jumped from the sixteenth floor to his death. It was reported as suicide. I lost my memory and became like a zombie. The secretary contacted cancer which spread throughout her body, she died from it. Remember the sign, "Enter at your own risk." I wrote many letters to Pastor Gate but to no avail. I also hired a lawyer and brought many foods and drinks for testing. Six different drugs were detected from sex drugs to mind controlling drugs. The treasure's wife who worked for a doctor provided the drugs to the church. Pastor Harry denied any wrong doing in a letter to me. In time the church became a cult. Sex orgies, especially among the youth, were common.

One of my friends, a church leader, left the church because of all those things. Pastor Harry was so upset. He ordered his son to retaliate. The son took some of his friends (young men and girls) to the home of my friend around midnight. They were armed with baseball bats and lots of rocks. The rocks were thrown through the windows, the bats came handy to smash the windshields of two cars parked outside. A big rock landed on the pillow where one of my friends' daughter was sleeping. She just had gone to the kitchen to drink a glass of water. The rock could have killed her. Two days later they came back to do more damage, again around midnight. My friend got sight of them and took the license plate number down. While interrogated by the police, Pastor Harry swore that the car (his son's boyfriend's car) in question was always parked in his own garage. Of course we all knew that he was lying. The damage amounted to over four thousand dollars (the insurance paid). The joke is this, "How many rocks does Pastor Harry carry in his car trunk?" He is a Palestinian. Rocks are part of their culture.

I wrote many letters to pastor Gate but to no avail. I also hired a lawyer and brought food and drinks for testing to her. Six different drugs were detected from sex drugs to mind altering drugs. The treasurer's wife who worked for a doctor provided the drugs to the church. In time the church became a cult. Sex orgies among the members especially among the youth were common. In my desperation I asked Jesus to remove Pastor Harry from the church. He left Canada a week later. I knew Pastor Gate would not leave no matter what. I asked the Holy Spirit to tell Pastor Gate that he had a ministry outside the church. Three days later he left telling people that the Holy Spirit told him that he had his own ministry outside the church. Things did not improve, so I left too. Recently Pastor Gate asked me for forgiveness (in a vision). "Of course," I said "you silly goose". My understanding was that he had died already or was going to die soon. He died soon after that. He died in a parking lot from a heart attack, just before boarding the bus he was driving.

By then the church had shrank from eight hundred members to a meager eighty. The finances had shrank too. The congregation was kicked out from the building for not being able to pay the lease. Some die hard have 'church' in a hotel ballroom with a new pastor.

I enrolled in a new church. The preaching seemed to be alright, but had no effect. Prophecies were off the wall and outright wrong.

One good thing came out of it. One Sunday a young couple accosted me, "Do not leave after the service we have things for you. I waited for them in the parking lot. I saw them picking up many grocery bags. Then they proceeded towards a very old car to unload the grocery bags. I motioned them to come to the car I was driving. It was an almost new Mercedes Benz. They looked shocked but tried not to let me know. After storing all the gifts in the trunk, the husband handed me an envelope. I took it thinking it might be a letter explaining their generosity. At home I opened the envelope. It contained a few hundred dollars. I felt really happy. The next Sunday I thanked the lady (her husband had to work) and asked her why they would do such a kind thing. "The Holy Spirit told us to give you the groceries and the money. You see we do not give any money to the church but to people like you." I gladly accepted the explanation. The pastor of that church left in disgrace. One of my friends dismissed the congregation and the pastor. Time again to move to another church.

Right from the beginning the Holy Spirit told me, "Pastor Holic is not to be trusted." By that He meant drugs in food or drinks. I was shocked. I made a covenant with Jesus. If drugs are used let the members leave and no new members come. We started the church with forty people. Unfortunately drugs were used to control the people. For my birthday one of the ladies baked a cake. I knew drugs were used but I trusted that lady. I ate a piece of the birthday cake. Instantly I felt the effects. My thyroid became impaired to the point where the heart beat fell to a dangerous level. Everybody who ate of the cake got sick too. You could tell it drained all energy from you. The next Sunday the pastor's wife presented a cake of her own. Surely I thought that cake must be safe to eat. It too had drugs in it. The leadership noticed the devastation the first cake had produced so this cake had the antidote baked in. The damage was already done. It proofed to me that the pastor, his wife and other church leaders were behind the drugging. I left that church. By then there were only sixteen members and a handful of floaters. A floater is a member who shows up about once per month. How dumb, how stupid, how idiotic and how deceived pastors can be. Do not become a pastor unless you have some common sense. There is no difference if you shoot a person or if you drug that person. In each case you destroy that person. Each time I enter a church I remind myself 'Enter at your own risk'. Rule #1 do not eat or drink in a church. I still face spiritual risks which may take days, weeks or months to recuperate from. The best remedy is to know your God.

Every Day Life Stresses

Any day of your life may be hazardous. Not only churches are hazardous but anywhere you go and park your life. Christians are very gullible, it comes with the territory. Therefore con artists make them their preferred target. Jesus told us to be wise as serpents and gentle as doves. "Therefore be as shrewd as snakes and as innocent as dove." (Matthew 10:16 NIV).

Stress is good for you, no stress no life. One must learn to handle stress and even to minimize stress. Someone invented a fifth season: Tis the Season. It lingers around Christmas and New Year. Many maximize their stress during 'Tis the Season'. Most heart attacks occur during that time. People eat more, drink more, do less and move less. Get some peace into your life and into the life of others. If you have a dog let him or her walk you more often during Tis the Season, you will not regret it I promise you.

Years ago I fell from a tree at the age of thirteen. The monkey manifested itself already at that early age. My father knew that I was climbing trees so he forbid me to climb any tree while he and Pedro were working the potatoes' fields. I got so bored, I had to climb a tree, thirty feet up. The rotten branches gave in under my weight and I crashed to the forest floor. Desperately I yelled and passed out. I recuperated quickly, nothing broken except my pride. A stern reproach from my father ringed in my ears for a while. Through most of my life back pain was the punishment of my disobedience. One wrong move and I was in pain. Occasionally the pain manifested itself during winter. If I was lucky I would slip on the ice. By trying to counterbalance the fall I would rearrange the spine and I would be o.k. again for awhile. One year during Tis I hurt my back so badly Fred had to drive me to a chiropractor. Bend over, moaning from pain I entered the doctor's office. Fifteen minutes later I reemerged, bend over more and in much greater pain. Fred asked me what had happened. I got treated by the chiropractor, a young grinning five foot short fellow. He repeatedly urged me to see a medical doctor. I was puzzled. Chiropractors never tell you to see a medical doctor. In any case he booked me for another appointment the next day. Fred drove me again the next day. I entered warped and twisted. A gentle tall guy greeted me, "What can I do for you?" "Who are you", was my response. "I am the chiropractor." "Who was here yesterday," I stammered. "That was the janitor, it was my day off." This time the chiro treatment helped and I got eventually well.

A couple of years ago an evangelist game to town. Occasionally I watched him on television. Lately it seemed he went off the wall with his teaching. Nevertheless I went to his meeting to see how far he went off the wall, a little or a lot? What he preached made sense, I was relieved. I had no problem standing in line for prayer except for my back pain. He prayed for me, I hit the floor. I got up, he prayed again, I hit the floor again. By now my back was healed and still is to this very day. God healed me in spite of my attitude or shall I say because of my bad attitude.

Doctors prescribed drugs are one of the leading causes of death. My brother's mother-in-law is the perfect example of that. She went to see her general practitioner in fairly good condition. After careful examination he convinced her that she might be sicker than she felt. He hospitalized her. Three weeks later she was dying and the doctor called her family to prepare for the funeral. He took her off all medication and no more food nor drink. She was unconscious too. One of her sons flew in from Jamaica. Lion had the task to pick him up at the airport. He told his wife, "Do not call me unless mother dies." Lion with the brother-in-law in his car raced on the highway to make certain the son could see his mother one more time before passing away. Then the phone rang. Lion thought we are too late, Florence must have died. Nevertheless he answered the call. "Lion, this is Florence, get me a bottle of wine and do not forget the scotch." Then she hung up. What had happened? Florence came to herself. Seeing all the wailing family members around her bed she send them home saying, "You are wasting your time I am not going to die get me Lion on the phone." She recovered from the drugs and continued to live but eventually neither wine nor scotch could keep her alive past one hundred.

Lion is a car salesman. Each time a prospective customer arrives he gets all excited. He cherishes to take them to a test drive, particularly young ladies. In the past a young fellow insisted to test drive by himself. He never returned. The car was found by the police weeks later. Ready to drive off he remembered that he forgot the dealer's plate. He left his cell phone on the dashboard and rushed back to his office. In no time he was back. His cell phone was gone by then. Again he dashed to his office. The cell phone was not to be seen. From the office he dialed his cell phone number hoping the ring would lead him to it. He came back to the parking lot where he saw a lady, the one he ought to give a test drive, jumping out of the car screaming, "A mouse in my panties, a mouse in my panties." It was not a mouse but Lion's cell phone set on vibration instead on ringing. The lady had stuffed the cell phone in her panties with the intention of stealing it. The test drive was no longer required.

Banks can cause you real problems, the employees that is not the buildings. There was this teller in training. She asked me politely, "Can I practice on you." She was very pretty, so I agreed enthusiastically. An hour later all the money from all my accounts had disappeared. Neither she nor I knew where it all went. Eventually days later it all returned but the teller was never to be seen again.

Cheques are quite expensive these days. I write them sparingly, the less cheques you write the more money stays in your account. It's that simple. Many businesses refuse to take cheques including the government. It's that bad. They all prefer credit cards. Cash is an even greater villain. When the government send back your cheques you know something is awfully wrong somewhere. But you still need to write the odd cheque. Particularly if you operate a business. Years ago I ordered new cheques. The bank teller gave me some free cheques, about a dozen or so, to tie me over in mean time. Occasionally I would inquire about them but the cheques never came. To heck with the cheques I said to myself. The bank can provide a dozen free cheques from time to time. That could save me hundreds of fidelies (dollars). But no, the teller told me no more free cheques, temporary cheques cost two dollar each. You never win with banks. Again I asked for the cheques I ordered. "When did you order them," the teller asked." "In November," I replied." "Sir, you must have more patience than that. This is only early December." "Oh, that was last year 2008 we are now 2009." That really rattled her. She ordered them anew. They arrived during the Tis season just before Christmas. Eagerly I opened the package. Horrified I noticed the misspelled company name. I phoned the cheque printing company to report the mistake. They apologized, and told me not to expect the new cheques any time soon. It will be sometimes next year. The following year 2010 they arrived, they were perfect. In meantime I managed to correct the misspelled name with a razor blade, they are good too now. I have to stay in business for another fifty years to make use of all the cheques. By the way they never asked for any money for any kind of cheques. I do not dare to tell them about it, they may request an arm and a leg for them.

Power failures are almost always a nuisance. Not so it seemed when you are in the bank. The tellers panic during such times. I experienced it by myself. I cashed in a cheque of a few hundred dollars just when the power went out. Some emergency lights came on like a faint moon. It gave some illumination. The teller gave me a bundle of bills. No need to count, I was certain it was the proper amount even though my wallet was bulging to the extreme. At home I counted four hundred too many. Days later I returned the loot. To my surprise the teller ask for more to return. She said, "We are still missing thousands of dollars." I denied her request, "Find another sucker please."

Most of the time you look forward to new appliances. May be not when it is you who has to pay for them. Some washer and dryer served you well over the years. So you look for the same make when your better half wants them replaced. Not that the old ones were not working anymore, oh no, just for the pleasure of new ones. Proudly I admired the new set of washer and dryer, they were like twins. It turned out the washer had a temperament. Depending on the cycle, the washer hopped, jumped, rattled and made the whole house vibrate. That much joy from a washer was definitely not needed. Close scrutiny revealed a damaged base. Someone must have attacked the washer in desperation. I had no problem in getting the washer replaced at no cost to me. The new washer was worse. It really moved around. The water hoses kept it from galloping to the next room. The company's complaint department insisted the floor was not sturdy enough for the washer to behave properly. They suggested I reinforce the floor. Easily said than done. I cut the floor open and build a fortress underneat. Proudly I started the washer, at last I thought. The floor no longer absorbed any vibration. It went from bad to worse, a lot worse. To all of my complaints I was told to read the manual. I did. There it was, "This washer can only be operated on a cement floor." Furious I dragged the beast to the garage. The beast was tamed, no side steps at all. That sealed its faith. It was returned to the store where I bought it and exchanged for one suitable for wooden floor. What an ordeal. The washer's mate, the dryer was fine, more than fine even a rat thought so. He intended to make his home inside. The rat managed to climb the wall outside, squeezed past the vent flap and there he was inside. Most likely he wanted to winter in a warm place. From time to time I heard him squeaking. I checked the troubles in the manufacturing guide but there was no mentioning of a rat. I was on my own. I figured if I unhook the vent pipe the rat will escape into the house which would be worse. At least I had him contained. There was only one thing to do: turn up the heat. For a while the rat was squealing and scratching, then it died down. Time to stop the procedure. The next day I heard again scratching. This time I turned the heat to the max and for some time. No more noise, I dragged the dyer to the outside and opened it up: no rat. He must have gone out the way he came in. I screwed the flap so no more rat visitor in the future.

Recently we were called to a doctor's residence for an electrical problem. The wife let us straight to the living room where a fat rat, belly up, adorned the carpet. He died of a drug overdose. Not very clever, you do not dine on medical supplies. The wife was outraged not at the rat but at her husband, the doctor. I want my husband to see this, you are my witnesses, he has to bury the rat.

Fridges too can be an ordeal. You can live without a washer for weeks but you will be hard pressed if your fridge kicks the bucket. It can also be very costly when all your fridge and freezer foods go limp. Reviving an old fridge is never a good idea. The fridge salesperson painted the devil on the wall to convince me to buy extra fridge life insurance. "Just in case," he said. The just in case happened six months down the road. All the foods spoiled. Because of the extra insurance I was compensated plus the repair was included. That repair failed a week later. It failed every consecutive week for the next four weeks. By then four different repairmen had worked on the fridge. The first one came back. He was determined to fix it once and for all. "I will cut the problem out, you do not need that part anyhow. If it does not work then dig a hole in your yard and bury the stinker." The fridge works perfectly ever since.

Work, Just Work

Everybody needs to work, sometimes. Most people die after retirement and those who do not die after retirement they are dead already. Scriptures tell us, "If you do not work, you should not eat." It only applies to those who do not want to work and not to those who want to work but cannot find a job.

Over the years people tried to pay us with different means: cash, cheques, credit cards, sex and marriage proposal. Some even paid us by cooking a meal for us. Others tried to avoid payment all together or delayed payment. Someone wrote us a cheque of thousands of dollars. I had my suspicion. I checked his bank to verify if there was enough funds to cover the cheque. There were ten dollars missing. I paid the ten dollars and got the cheque certified before going to my bank to cash it. Cheques really have a life of their own. A lady send her cheque by mail. Unfortunately I opened the envelope in the landry room. The cheque fell into a crevice of the washer and no matter how hard I tried to retrieve I could not find it. I asked the lady to send me a new cheque. She gladly did so. No cheque arrived for weeks. Finally I phoned and asked about it. "Oh," she said, "the mail box got vandalized. Would you like me to send you another one." "Please, no I will pick it up in person."

A reputable company's cheque was late. I inquired politely. To my surprise I was told that the cheque writing machine had broken down. So much for cheque writing machines. Today computers do the trick, the cheques I mean.

When the government wants to pay you with a credit card then there is something wrong with the government system. We did some maintenance work for the landlord who leased the premises to the government. While working there we were ask to do some work for the government itself. We send the invoice to the government. Six months passed and still no sign of the payment. If you are late in paying taxes the government is quick at your heels and make you pay with hefty penalties. I requested payment and was told that they lost the invoice. I faxed them another one. Two weeks later while sitting at my desk I got a call from Ottawa. "Do you take credit card payment." "No, I waited long enough, send me a cheque." The government cheque finally made it to our mail box. Next time we were working at that government place, the engineer who handled our invoice told us the whole story while laughing himself to pieces. Armed with my faxed invoice he flew to Ottawa. He wrote a two page report in regards to the work we invoiced the government. He also asked for payment. The government clerk phoned me at that time and told the engineer Peacock is the problem. What a waste of time and money. The engineer flew especially to Ottawa to write the report, he overnighted in a hotel and returned back to Vancouver the next day all expenses paid by no other than the government. The invoice amounted to sixty nine dollars and seventy cents. Who is the problem: Peacock or the government?

In Ottawa the members of parliament congregate at times from building to building, rain or shine. That was a good thing, a very good thing especially during the winter months. One day someone in the government came up with a crazy idea to build an underground tunnel so that the members would be no longer exposed to the cold weather. It has a great drawback for the tax payers. Up to that point the politicians had their hands at least sometime in their own pockets. Now they have their hands in the taxpayers' pockets all the time.

Cats and dogs were created to make life more bearable for the human race. Sometimes people forget that thought. Not everybody likes a dog in the living room. Now you can have the benefit of a dog in your living room without having a dog. For about three thousand dollars you can buy a table for your living room. It has a leg raised up in the air (like a dog raising his leg for urinating against a tree) a metal stem (the urine) to sturdy the table at the raised leg location with a metal puddle at the floor (representing the urine puddle). No mess, no stink, what a great idea!

In long line up at the bank I wish I had a dog with me. In one of those very long line ups I noticed a lady with her dog: a great big dog. For a dog, his behavior was exceptional. Half an hour through the waiting that changed drastically. First the dog manifested an uneasy behavior followed by a noisy search for a place, he only knew what place. Then the manager called me to her desk to expedite the long line up more quickly. I told the manager unless you serve the lady with the dog immediately, he, the dog will make a deposit you may not like. The manager rushed to the dog. Too late, he had already made a deposit of poop.

Trying to select the best dish from the menu in a restaurant can take time. What do I choose: beef, chicken or seafood? While deliberating in my mind I noticed the cook (chef hat on) bringing in a dead cat from the street. The cat just was run over by a car. The cook disappeared with the cat in the kitchen. Soon afterwards the waiter appeared at my table. He greatly recommended a rabbit dish. He had nothing but praise for the rabbit dish. Rabbit was not even on the menu. I quickly opted for seafood that night. I think I never regretted it. Don't you think so?

Crawl spaces and attics are good friends of electricians. They made it easy to add any kind of wiring throughout the house. To access those places is another story. One of our customers had his access to the crawlspace under the kitchen sink.

I tried to wiggle myself through the hole. The customer left the house and told us to lock the door when we leave. It was noontime. The sandwich in my pocket prevented me from making it through the opening. I decided to have lunch while standing with my feet on the floor of the crawlspace with my upper body just under the sink. I was looking out to the kitchen. Was my ham sandwich ever so good. I was horrified when a huge dog came towards me. He growled, showing off his big teeth. I had no chance in winning this one. I handed my delicious sandwich to the dog. He disappeared the same way he appeared never to be seen again. I made it easily through the floor opening.

Fred and me worked for an old lady. She complained about the price we quoted her for her job. "It is too low, far too low," she kept saying. That was a first. It could be very easily corrected to our delight. We love complaints like that. She always was escorted by her cat and her medium size dog. What a trio!

At four o'clock the cat and the dog jumped on the couch in the living room facing the television. Then the doorbell rang. The cat and the dog were expecting their friend. Their friend was a huge dog. He too jumped on the couch. All the animals looked at the television then at the old lady. She understood. She joined them on the couch and turned on the television. Of course they wanted to see their favorite game show. From time to time depending on the action on the screen the dogs would growl and nod their heads. It was too funny for us to see those animals. We lost concentration and as a result the big chandelier we were about to install crushed to the floor. The glass shade shattered into thousands of pieces. It was not the broken chandelier that upset the animals but the noise we made. They were very annoyed. We had to buy a new shade out of our own pockets, but the price was right. We even got a substantial discount from the lighting store by telling the sales person about the animals.

A famous motivational speaker came to town from California. He had prepared his speech but he could not find an appropriate title. On his way to Vancouver he was sitting beside Dolly Parton. Like every man he glanced at Dolly from time to time. All of a sudden he got the title to his speech: think big, think very big.

We in the Western World take toilets for granted. Only when they clog up we notice how important they are to our daily living. One of our customer went sightseeing Japan. On her return she asked us if we would like to see her photo album from her Japan trip. Excited we said, "Yes, of course." We expected the famous Japanese rock gardens. But no, all had picture from toilets, a lot of toilets, hundreds of them. After viewing all those toilet pictures she proudly announced, "Would you like to touch my seat? It is nice and warm." Startled, we thought she would like us to touch her naked bum. What she meant was to touch her toilet seat, a computerized toilet seat. It replaces the old fashion bidets. I could not help and asked, "How much did it cost?" "Eighteen hundred dollars, worth every penny," she beamed. "That's a real bum deal," I gasped. Another customer found great delight in his toilet seat. He encouraged everyone to made use of his toilet. His toilet seat was a clear plastic with threatening fish hooks embedded in it. I tried it, it sent shivers through my spine.

There is hardly any household which does not have at least one television set. Television time can be very relaxing if sprinkled with your favorite snacks. During those highlights while enjoying the snacks you do not want to miss out on any action. You just stuff the wrappers under the couch. You will be found out, believe me. My friend Joe was one of those culprits. Repeated warnings from his wife fell on deaf ears. Joe continued to accumulate his snack wrappers under the couch. Last time he did that, he got the surprise of his life. While putting a wrapper under the couch, his fingers got caught in a mouse trap. His wife had placed it there on purpose. He screamed of course. Now he understood why his wife had asked him, a few days ago, to buy some mouse cheese. It worked, Joe is finally cured from his behavior thanks to his lovely wife who had such a bright idea. A good way to change your husband.

How the local economy is doing is reflected in the way our customers treat us. We were contracted to install a few light fixtures in a penthouse of a downtown highrise building. The owner announced solemnly, "Before you do any work here are the rules you have to abide by. No drinking on the job. That include water, juices or soft drinks. If you drink, you have to pee and I do not pay for pee time." Obviously the economy was not doing too well at that time.

You cannot please all the people all the time. Even though you do your best to please the customer. There are times it just does not happen. We worked so hard at this particular place. We strived to finish the job that day. It meant we worked late into the evening. Fred was mudding the final touch. I was standing beside the owner facing a long corridor. Then a totally naked lady appeared at the end of the hallway. She shouted, "Al, come to bed, right now." She was the owner's wife. First I thought it must be a fata morgana. I closed my eyes, hoping the apparition would be still there when I open my eyes again. The fata morgana was still there. Eventually she vanished, to reappear dressed in a night gown. Al, her husband thanked her for showing herself naked. Before I could conceive a judgmental opinion about the couple, God the Father scolded me, "You pray for them, they are my children." They had been drinking a lot of wine that evening. Lesson learnt: do not judge people or you will have no time to love them.

There are different kind of people living in government subsidized housing. We were called to repair a dining room chandelier in such a housing complex. The tenant, an older lady greeted us very kindly. After we repaired the chandelier, she urged us to have some food. Work time half an hour, eating time two hours. She dished us up what the table could hold. Soon we realized that the old lady was lonely, very lonely. We did not mind to keep her company for a while. Days later we were called in again to replace the repaired chandelier with a new one. Again the lady dished out whatever you could muster. She insisted that she did not like the new chandelier. Again we were called in to replace the chandelier with a metal shade. Apparently the glass shade shattered. The truth is the old lady hit it with her cane hoping we would come again to keep her company. We bought a new chandelier with a metal shade and made arrangement to get it installed. We rang the bell, but nobody answered. We waited for two hours, then left disappointed. I called the manager to complain that we had no access to the apartment. I said, "It is terrible." "So you heard, the old lady died while you were ringing the bell." A good thing we were involved in doing the electrical work for her otherwise nobody would have found her, possibly for weeks. We had made the appointment with her son, who lived elsewhere. He forgot to tell his mother that we were coming. May be she would have lived a bit longer.

Ringing the doorbell is a very important procedure before entering a stranger's home. We had an appointment in a basement suite. We were late that day. We hang a chandelier, a very heavy one. The ceiling had to be reinforced for it to hold the heavy load. Of course we had to ask for forty dollars extra. Money the owner did not have. The customer refused to pay any extra but suggested his wife could cook a meal for us. We accepted gladly. We were hungry it took us a while eating hence we were late to the next appointment. The landlord let us in the basement suite and took off. Out of nowhere a dripping naked lady (the tenant) appeared screaming her head off. We quickly calmed her down explaining her that we were the electricians, the late electricians. "I give you twenty minutes then you must be out of here," she stammered. Fair enough we thought. Fred exclaimed, "This is hard work, what have we done to deserve punishment like this?" Our intention was to run a cable through her bedroom, but that was out of the question now. Instead we poked a hole through the wall and installed the cable in the furnace room.

Living in a multi million dollars home is not always the best. You do not always get what you pay for. This house had no doorbell. When the house was build the doorbell was forgotten. You can have a wireless doorbell, but that may cause another problem. In this case the maid unplugged the chime with the receiver end and disposed of it because the doorbell never worked. She never thought of replacing the battery in the door button. The owner's business friend from Australia came to visit. He pressed the door button, nothing happened. Thinking his friend was not at home he returned to Australia, very disappointed. He left his cellular phone at home because of airport safety concern. The property was gated with a high fence. When the owner heard about his friend misfortune he commissioned his brother-in-law, an architect to get a wired doorbell installed. He called us, we did not wanted to do the job. The house was surrounded by concrete walkways, very difficult to run a wire for the door bell. But it could be done. Every tree had sprinklers for fire protection. How much is the owner willing to pay for the doorbell? That was the question. "As long as you do not shock the billionaire you can go ahead with the work." "Fine, how about one thousand dollars," I said. "Ok, we have a deal." Can you imagine thousand dollars for a doorbell! We grooved the concrete of the sidewalks and sealed it after the bell wire was installed. The bell worked perfectly. The billionaire has other problems. You take a shower in that house if the computer who dispenses the hot water does not like you, you only get cold water. The billionaire's wife contacted pneumonia, she had to be hospitalized. The billionaire himself drove across town to his friend for a hot shower. How does that strike you? Be happy in your modest home and enjoy a good warm shower.

The times are long gone when you wanted to hammer your computer. In those days the computers came with a manual. Now it is all in the computer. The thing is you must know how to turn on the computer. My friend with a very high IQ took two days to figure out how to turn his laptop on. You see just pressing the on button did not do the trick. You must press it for some time. It took me two hours to turn the laptop on. Understandably because I was struck by lightning at a tender age. I was greatly tempted to hammer it right then and there.

Shopping at a store where they advertise that they will beat any Price can be very hazardous if your last name is Price. So be pre-warned, do not tell anybody unless you need a spanking.

Fluorescent energy saving's tubes give you less light, they also fail a lot quicker. One of our customer realized where the savings come in. "They give you less light, you need more fixtures. The saving comes when they fail and the electricians take a long time to replace them."

Trade inspectors and city official can make life miserable for homeowners and trades men. We worked at a customer's place who expected city officials to inspect his premises. He did not have yet a building permit, hence we were unable to get an electrical permit. We had to work there because it was to dangerous to let the energized wires just dangling about. We ought to disappear and take a break when the officials were in the wind. They were late and surprised us. The customer's wife quickly pushed us in a closet and locked the door. We heard him offer a case of beer to every official then bars of chocolate. They all refused. In the end he got the approval he was looking for and we got paid for closet time.

It took one of our customers quite a while, after the initial start up, to continue building his commercial mall. By then the regulations had changed. Earthquake proof rules were in place and disabled toilets (for impaired persons) were mandatory. The plumbing for the toilets were in the wrong location in regards to the wall. The customer reaped a heap of hassle from all the inspectors in particular from the building inspector. A long weekend came up at that time. He encouraged us to work that weekend. He himself opted to take a vacation to the North end of the Vancouver Island. He wanted to relax at a secluded Bed and Breakfast place. We worked thirty six hours in a row to make up time to ready the job for power connection. When he came back from the retreat I asked, "How was it? Are you well relaxed now?" He grinned and said, "You will not believe what happened. The only two persons at the Bed and Breakfast were the building inspector and me. He too was fed up, he too needed a well deserved break. We had three days to ourselves to iron out our differences." From then on the dealings with the inspector went smoothly. But the city was determined to make the life of our customer totally miserable. He sold ten acres to a farmer, who in turn sold it to a developer. Here is the catch: If you develop two acres, the city will pay for the roads and the utilities. The developer created five companies, each developing two acres. It is legal to give a gift of seven thousand dollars to each counselor including the mayor. A nice way to pave the road ahead. Plans were drawn up, roads and houses were built. To our customer's horror, one road ended smack against one of his commercial building. Any tourist could see a unique attraction: a building in the middle of a road (Schildburger development). Our customer took the developer and the city to court, even the high court. In each case he lost. Not only did he lose but the judge muzzled him with a gag order not to slander the developer nor the city. Further he was order by the same judge to pay for any legal costs of the city and of the developer. It amounted to two hundred twenty thousand dollars not counting his own legal costs. Next the city raised his property taxes from fifty thousand dollars to one hundred fifty thousand dollars. It was adding insult to injury. He pleaded with the city official to buy him out. Their response was simple, "We do not buy you out, we take it as soon as you try to do something with your property." He could not raise the lease for the tenants, it just was too big of a tax raise. In his desperation he called on a friend, a realtor. In his mind he thought he might get five hundred thousand dollars at the most for the commercial property. The realtor assessed the property at four million dollars. Our customer thought that's highway robbery. May be three millions will do. Not so, in the end he got four millions, time to stick out the tongue at the city officials.

Some people think by calling a non-trades man will safe them a lot of money. It most likely give them a lot of troubles as well. This lady bought a chandelier from a local store. She asked her neighbor to install it. He gladly obliged. He also installed a dimmer. He turned the power on. Everything lit up real good but only for a moment then half the apartment went dark. Obviously there was something wrong somewhere. She called the manger of the apartment complex. The manger sent her a tile layer who happened to work there that day. The tile layer reconfigured the wiring, installed a new dimmer and power everything up. This time it lit up with a big bang and plunged the whole apartment into darkness. No television watching for the teenage son. Time for him to take matters in his own hands. Armed with a screwdriver he poked around in the double switch box. He forgot to turn the remaining power off. He was epileptic and had a seizure at that very moment. It sizzled and sparked. Absolute total darkness followed. Good for him, the screwdriver had an insulated handle. On the other hand, if shocked it may have cured him. Our customer again called on the property manager. We were called and corrected all the mistakes plus the short in the chandelier. She paid a pretty penny for the chandelier including the short it came with.

Another customer had a new towel bar installed. Each time anybody touched that towel bar was shocked real good. We found out that the towel bar installer used a three inch screw to fasten it. The screw went straight through an electrical cable. The towel bar was energized with one hundred twenty volts. The gyproc acted as insulator therefore the circuit breaker did not de-energized that circuit. It was fortunate that there were no horses around, it would have killed them. Horses are very sensitive to electric shock. We told the tenant to look at the bright side for not being a horse. She was not amused. Some people just do not have a humorous vein.

Sooner or later everybody has to make a trip to the dentist. We went as electricians. Electrical things had to be fixed. The patients were in the dental chair while I was going back and forth with my tool pouch on and a power drill in my hand. A man was reclined in the dental chair. Nervously he observed me. He thought that I was the dentist. When a patient adjacent to him screamed, he panicked. He tried to escape but two dental assistants held him down. They convinced him that I was not the dentist but the friendly electrician.

We installed daylight fluorescent tubes for a customer by mistake. He wanted cool white. "Are you replacing them?" he asked. "Not really", I replied. "If you do not replace them right now I will beat the daylight out of you. Is that clear?"

Clear enough and so much for daylight tubes.

A little boy, about five years old, let us in the apartment to do some electrical work. The door did not fully open , there was too much stuff behind. The stove had three feet of things piled on top of the heating elements. The beds too carried a lot of stuff about half way to the ceiling. The mother was still sleeping on the couch at noontime. You could not move an inch without bumping into something. We had to move some boxes. The boy reminded us to place them exactly where they were before, so he could find his things when he needed them. The carpet was a very dirty black. I moved the legs of the dining room table just a little to see the carpet's original color. It was white. The little boy had one more request from us, "Sir, please remove your shoes." I liked his attitude. Among all the filth he yearned for cleanliness, law and order. The human nature years for holiness, do not suppress it.

Small businesses may have hard times. Job opportunities are like jo-jos. At times you have too many jobs to handle and other times dry periods. We decided to have another company name beside our original name. The same workers, the same location except we had now two names. We expected double the calls, extra jobs at no extra costs. As soon as we advertized under the new name, collection agencies came after us. We had chosen a name of a company that did not exist anymore. Unpaid bills too made their way to our mailbox. Then a woman called and addressed me as Harry. I tried my best to convince her that that was not my name. "Don't play dumb with me. Can you pick up your pants." "What pants?" I retorted. "The pants you left behind when my husband suddenly came home and you jumped out the window leaving your pants behind." Next the inspection department got on our case. According to them you cannot have two companies unless you have different people to staff them. The new name gave us a lot of grief but no work. We opted out but before we did the previous owner of that company threatened to sue us unless we pay him thirty thousand dollars.

You may leave home for work happy as a lark but you never know what that day will dish up for you. An elderly lady, or should I say a mature lady called us to check out her chandelier. She was concerned one link may open, possibly a first sign of a crash. We rang the bell but no answer. At that moment a young woman, a tenant, of that apartment complex came out. I stretched my hand forward to prevent the door from closing. The lady screamed, "You thief, you are not going in and rob us again." She clenched her fist with her door keys in it and hammered my chest. In self defense I let go the door. Instinctively I put a neck hold on her and squeezed her strongly. She yelped, "Help, help." People just

laughed at her. Fred said as a matter of fact, "Let her go. She is trouble." And trouble she was. I let her go and we went to our van. Three bodybuilders ran towards the van. Quickly we locked all the doors. We tried to drive off. They pulled their pickup behind us. We were in a mousetrap. They also called the police. We breathe a sigh of relieve when we heard the siren. We both intended to jump out from the van but the police with drawn guns told us otherwise. Each with hands up in the air, slowly moved from the van. The tazers were not yet invented. We were glad for that. The lady told the officers that I attacked her viciously. The police sided with the lady and were determined to handcuff me and drag me off to the jail. We called our lawyer at a cost of four hundred fifty dollars were set free. Three weeks later my home was burglarized. The police came and asked us if we had insurance. I said, "Yes." The officer closed her book, end of the investigation. By then my chest was bruised and very pain full. I mentioned to the officer what had happened to me and complained about the way I was treated by the police. I even indicated the police officer. "We had problems with that officer before," she retorted. She also urged me to go to the hospital for x-ray. I went on the spot and waited for the result. Grimfaced the doctor told me, "Mr. Peacock you have lung cancer." I was shocked. Then he noticed that I was short build and that the x-ray of the chest did not matched my build. He disappeared for a while. "There was a mistake in marking the x-ray. Your name was put on somebody else's x-ray and vice-versa. We just send home that fellow, telling him that he has a bruised rib. It is you that has a bruised rib and the other fellow has the lung cancer. Sorry for the confusion."

Sometimes you have to be your own detective. I noticed rather quickly that my garbage bags were not collected. The rule is clear: two bags per household per week. If there are more bags you must attach a five dollars coupon to each additional bag. I was on the lookout. Amazingly four bags adorned my driveway. Two were my own and two were stray bags. First I phoned the city and was told to call the police unless the bags lay on city property. The police advised me to get the license plate of the vehicle and then hire a lawyer. To me this was all nonsense. I had a better idea: become a garbage detective. I emptied the stray bags on the garage floor. Now the investigation could start. The treasure hunt was on. The bag content belonged to a young couple of a suburb. She was breastfeeding. They lived on pizzas, coke and similar junk food. His pay cheque slip revealed his place of work (not far from where I lived) his address, his name and the amount of pay. Even their names were found on paid bills. I called their home. A lady answered. To me it was clear, her husband dropped their garbage at my place on his way to work every week. I explained everything to her. She was outraged, "So that's what he does with our garbage." I requested that her husband picks up their garbage on his way home that same day. He did and left me a note of apology in the mail box. I was surprised, possibly he spent

sometime in the dog house. A good ending to a messy incident. Police, lawyers or the city are not always the solution.

False alarms, burglar alarms can be costly. The local city officials fine you severely for the police to attend to false alarms. Who is to say what is a false alarm? One cloudy day I came home. I noticed my outdoor lights were on and a police cruiser was parked across the street. My outdoor lights work on a string, a pull string that is. You pull the string: the lights come on, you pull again the lights go out (high tech for an electrician). I always thought that my alarm was fool proof. It went off, my neighbor (very helpful) called the police. When I pulled the string nothing happened. The alarm display indicated that a possible intruder tried to visit me. I called 911. "How many burglars are there?" I was asked. "They left already," I stammered. "Good, hang up and call the regular police number, do not clog the system." I follow the instructions. A week later a nasty bill of one hundred and seven dollars was send to me for the 'false alarm'. This was not a false alarm. I had the proof: a broken pull chain switch. I replaced that switch the same day. Numerous attempts to get the charge removed failed. The city clerk made fun of me and promised that I would never win with the city. Their record proofed it. Through my investigation I found out that one of the officers had pulled the string and broke the switch. Aha, the police is the guilty one. Instantly I send the police a bill of ninety five dollars, labour and material plus taxes. That bill made the police sergeant spring into action. On the phone he told me, "We never had a case like this, we do not know how to handle this. We normally do not pay bills!!!!! Is it possible that a real intruder pulled the string and broke the switch. Then the police officer, a lady, very gently pulled the same string. (by then I was wondering what string he intended to pull on me?) In other words a real prospective burglar broke your switch. I will tear up the invoice with your permission. Further I will instruct the city to cancel the fine." I agreed. There was but one problem. My daughter paid the fine on my behalf as a Valentine's gift. I raced to the city hall. The clerk was no longer laughing and they had to reimburse my daughter. I broke their record. Do not be intimidated by either the city or the police, stand up for what is right.

Coloring books used to be for toddlers only. Think again, apparently coloring books is of great benefits for university students as well. One of the local university prides itself to give a course in anatomy. Every student is required to color a book (only one hundred twenty pages) of anatomic organs inside and outside the body. It begs for great talent, every student is graded for it. To color the male and female private parts in exotic colors may be hilarious, but past page eighty you will experience sore fingers. Still it is good to practice early in life.

I like to do research at the university library. Sometimes I fall asleep on a couch. The other day I was poked out of my nap by the security. They told me in words and gestures, "No sleeping only studying here." They also offered me a cigarette. I kindly refused, because I do not smoke. They thought I was a bum. Giving me a cigarette was a nice way to get rid of me, no smoking in public places.

The mystery of the proverbial stiff upper lip of the British is finally solved: botox.

I needed botox for one of my teeth. A root canal had to be redone. After poking inside my tooth for an hour, my dentist decided to send me to a specialist for the root canal because he could not find the nerves. The secretary phoned me the day before my appointment. "Do you know what the specialist is doing?" "Not really," I gasped "He is cleaning one of your molars, it will cost you two thousand dollars. Do not worry we do accept any credit card." I was shocked to the extreme. I really did not want to lose my tooth. The specialist worked on me for about half an hour then he declared, "Your tooth has to be extracted." He sent me back to my regular dentist. I paid four hundred fifty dollars to be told that my tooth had to be extracted. My dentist refused to extract the tooth which was my unspoken wish. Even today my molar is doing what it is supposed to do: bite and grind food.

Recently the battery of my wristwatch had to be replaced. While waiting for that to be done a tradesman walk in the jewelry store. "Do you have any tradesman watches for sale?" "What kind of a watch is that, I never heard of it," replied the jeweler." "It is a watch that advances an extra ten minutes per hour. It means you make extra money when paid by the hour," grinned the tradesman.

There are times when things just do not turn out the way you want them to turn out. Your patience is tempted to the utmost. Those are the periods when things fall apart. I experience a period like that. The septic tank clogged up, so did the soap box, the garage door broke, the drive way caved in, the roof on the garage and on the barn leaked so badly both had to be replaced, the muffler fell off, the microwave breathe its last, the wheel barrow's tire became holed (twelve holes), the bolt holding the lawn mower's blade snapped. I quickly used an older lawn mower. After a while it became so noisy even with protective earmuff. First I thought this is very good my hearing has improved greatly. Then I found the muffler lying in the grass. There went my hearing improvement. How sad. The unexpected happened next: the lawn mower broke in half. The handle, two wheels and part of the body made up one piece, the motor, two wheels and the remaining part of the body the other piece. The motor was still running, but it did me no good.

There are times when time is against you. The days just do not have enough hours only twenty four, why not twenty six? That would really help you. I turned around and around on a parking lot but only the lot for disabled persons was empty. All I needed was ten minutes, ten lousy minutes. I took it. I hardly turned the engine off when out of nowhere the parking lot attendant popped up. "Sir, you cannot park here unless my buddy over there (a body builder type) roughs you up real good. You will be disabled alright and the entitlement to park here is guaranteed. I politely declined and looked for a less hostile spot.

An elderly lady (eighty five and counting) asked for an electrical estimate. On my way back to the car she shouted from her balcony, "Do not get lost." She might as well has said, "Get lost." Because she never called me back to get the work done, not until a year later. "You come now it is urgent," she begged on the phone. "What's the rush all of a sudden," I dared to question. "My apartment and all the other apartments of the complex are teaming with bedbugs. Do not come alone, bring at least another person with you, the more the better." In her opinion the more people work there the less bugs are left, once the workers are gone. "When are the exterminators fumigating your apartment," I asked. "I do not know, nobody knows. The exterminators want to surprise the bedbugs, because it is not good for the bedbugs to know in advance when they are exterminated." Makes sense or does it?

All incidents, all influences in anybody's life must become a resource and cease to be a control. If that happens that person will be a great success and will enjoy life to its full.

It is time to go back to faith. Here is the latest slogan to witness to unbelievers. Christians used to witness to unbelievers by asking them, "Are you Christian? Would you like to become a Christian?" Then it was changed to, "Are you born again? You must be born again or you go to hell." People would come to me and ask, "Are you one of those born again weirdoes? If yes then get away from me." The 'born again' advocates realized that it was not a good approach so they changed it to 'coming to faith'. That poses even greater problems. Asking a Muslim, a Buddist, a Hindu or any other person of faith that question and you will get the same answer: yes. But are they Christians? Of course not. It defeats the purpose. My friend Joe's wife is called Faith. He is not a Christian but he watched a Christian program on television. At one point the preacher urged everyone to 'come to Faith'. Joe jumped up and shouted, "You perverts get your own wife."

Over the years I have seen many false statements by preachers and Christians alike. All will weaken the listeners and prevent them from maturing spiritually and otherwise. It is time to take a fresh look, without prejudice, at the Christian faith, the Christian belief system.

Identity Problem in the Church

Deception was the downfall of Adam and Eve. Even today deception is the downfall of many. It is the greatest evil of all times. Adam and Eve were created in the image and likeness of God, they were like God. God's DNA was pulsating through their whole being. They did not know good and evil, they lived under grace and not under law. They were totally innocent and holy, clothed in God's righteousness and holiness. Not knowing good and evil, they were unable to sin. They had a free will but they had no choice to choose either good or evil. God warned them for their own good.

Satan was jealous of them. God had given Adam and Eve power and authority over the created earth and over everything on it. Satan had lost that authority when he fell. The original earth was destroyed at that time. Satan put doubt in the mind of Adam and Eve of who they were. He promised them that they would surely not die and become like God. Eve wanted something good: to become like God, nothing evil or bad. The problem was that they were already like God. They had an identity problem. "You will not surely die," the serpent said to the woman." For God knows that when you eat of it your eyes will be opened; and you will be like God." (Gen. 3:4-5 NIV).

Fear entered their beings for the first time. "I heard you in the garden, and I was afraid because I was naked; so I hid. (Gen. 3:10 NIV). Faith in God was shattered, they believed Satan instead of God. The damage was done. All their offspring will be born a stillbirth and no one will be able to lift himself or herself out of the quagmire by cheer performance on their own. Only the Son of Man will be able to do that for all humanity.

When Jesus came on the scene, again Satan attacked His identity. The temptation had to do with Jesus and who He was. It was somehow trickier than for Adam and Eve. You could almost say it was reversed. Adam and Eve were made in the image and likeness of God, Jesus was God made in the image and likeness of men. If Satan would have succeeded in tricking Jesus to act as the Son of God, His mission to save humanity would have failed. Only as a man, the second Adam, the Son of Man could He restore humanity to its former glory. Jesus had to act as the Son of Man and not as the Son of God. This He had to do not only while He was tempted but throughout His entire earthly life as the Son of Man. Jesus knew who He was: the Son of God. He did not have to prove it to anybody. Satan repeatedly tempted Him. "If you are the Son of God…do this, do that." Jesus as the Son of Man did not fall in Satan's trap. "If you are the Son of God, tell these stones to become bread." "If you are the Son of God," he said, "throw yourself down." (Matthew 4:3,6 NI).

In the Church many have lost their true identity. Satan is still out there to deceive the born of God believers in who they really are.

What is the Identity of a Born of God Believer?

Everybody is born in the natural a sinner. We all are offspring of Adam and Eve. In God's eye we are born a stillbirth: dead spirit, mind and body. Some believe since we move, breathe and live a natural life, think and act, we are only spiritually dead. If that was the case then our physical body could still be a seed, the seed to a glorified body and with that body we would have access to heaven. The truth is as a sinner we are eternally separated from God.

Characteristics of the Original Spirit, Mind and Body

1) They were made in the image and likeness of God, created in a higher class than angels or any other creature—perfect, whole and mature in spirit, mind and body. "Do you not know that we will judge angels?"(1 Corinthians 6:3 NIV).

    "Are not all angels ministering spirits sent to serve those who will inherit   salvation (Hebrews 1:14NIV).

2) The spirit was made out of the very essence of God, the mind and body were made from the dust of the ground.

3) The spirit was born of God with God's very life in him and her, the dwelling place of God Almighty. The mind and body enjoyed divine health and beauty. Beauty and health is part of God Himself. Since mankind was created in the image and likeness of

God, it is understood that those attributes were part of Adam and Eve.

4) The spirit, mind and body were immortal and eternal. The original immortality was conditional to Adam's obedience to God. "And the Lord God commanded the man, 'You are free to eat from any tree in the garden; but you must not eat from the tree of knowledge of good and evil, for when you eat of it you will surely die'" (Genesis 2:16–17 NIV).

5) The spirit had the ability to make free choices and to make personal decisions; a totally free will. The mind and body were able to choose and to do freely whatever their desires were, including to eat or not to eat from the tree of knowledge of good and evil. The conscience gave clear guidance.

6) The spirit, mind and body had total and complete dominion and authority on and over the whole earth. "…let them rule over the fish of the sea and the birds of the air, over the livestock, over all the earth, and over all the creatures that move along the ground" (Genesis 1:26 NIV).

7) The spirit, mind and body were not affected by time or space.

8) The spirit, mind and body operated in perfect faith. The heart (not the physical heart but the heart as part of the spirit) and mind were one—single minded.

9) They walked in the spirit, in perfect love and fellowship with God.

10) In everything, they were blessed and not cursed. "God blessed them" (Genesis 1:28 NIV).

The Bible does not tell us how long Adam and Eve lived the perfect life in the Garden of Eden. They were not subjected to sickness or disease, but pain, as a protective measure, was part of that perfect life. "To the woman he said, "I will greatly increase your pains in childbearing" (Genesis 3:16 NIV). For pain to be increased, it had to be there in the first place. But when Adam and Eve disobeyed God, they suffered the consequences and their perfect life came to an end.

The Fall of Humankind

> Now the serpent was more crafty than any of the wild animals the Lord God had made. He said to the woman, "Did God really say, 'You must not eat from any tree in the garden'?"

> The woman said to the serpent, "We may eat fruit from the trees in the garden, but God did say, 'You must not eat fruit from the tree that is in the middle of the garden, and you must not touch it, or you will die.'"
>
> "You will not surely die," the serpent said to the woman. "For God knows that when you eat of it your eyes will be opened, and you will be like God, knowing good and evil."
>
> When the woman saw that the fruit of the tree was good for food and pleasing to the eye, and also desirable for gaining wisdom,[something good in itself] she took some and ate it. She also gave some to her husband, who was with her, and he ate it. Then the eyes of both were opened, and they realized they were naked; so they sewed fig leaves together and made coverings for themselves (Genesis 3:1–7 NIV).

We do not know how long Adam and Eve lived the perfect life before they were deceived by the craftiness of Satan, but the moment they disobeyed, disaster struck. Instantly they died spiritually, God's life was no longer in them. Fear entered their hearts for the first time. No longer did they operate in faith, but in fear—Satan's mode of operation. Their spirit was still made out of the essence of God, but was deprived of God's life. In God's eye that is death. From that point, all Adam's offspring would be born of the flesh and not born of God. Every offspring would be born with a dead spirit, a spiritual stillbirth and their physical body was no longer a seed for a glorified body. But the damage did not stop there. Satan was cursed, Eve was cursed, Adam was cursed, all their offspring were cursed and the earth was cursed.

Who is Satan? To answer that question one has to go back in history. Satan is one of the three known archangels. Archangels are the chiefs, the leaders and rulers. We know three of them: Michael, Gabriel and Lucifer (Satan).

Lucifer, an archangel full of wisdom and of perfect beauty, who was anointed leader of worship, ruled over the earth as well as the heavenly powers and the demons. Jealousy, pride and rebellion entered his heart, and he said,

> I will ascend into heaven; I will exalt my throne above the stars of God; I will sit upon the mount of the congregate; I will ascend above the height of the clouds; I will be like the Most High (Isaiah 14:13–14 NIV paraphrased).

The result was disastrous. Lucifer was cast out from the third heaven to the second heaven. He does not live on the earth, but he visits a lot. He rules from his place of authority. The heavenly powers that rebelled with him (one third of the angels) fell with him. Although Lucifer was hurled to the earth and expelled from the third heaven, he was not banished from the second heaven: his place of authority. Daniel describes heavenly warfare, and in Ephesians we see spiritual forces of evil in action in heavenly realms.

> But the prince of the Persian kingdom resisted me twenty-one days. Then Michael, one of the chief princes, came to help me, because I was detained there with the king of Persia (Daniel 10:13 NIV).

> For our struggle is not against flesh and blood, but against the rulers, against the authorities, against the powers of this dark world and against the spiritual forces of evil in the heavenly realms (Ephesians 6:12 NIV).

"How you have fallen from heaven, O morning star, son of the dawn! You have been cast to the earth, you who once laid low the nations!" (Isaiah 14:12 NIV). At his fall, the original earth, once ruled by Lucifer, experienced the fall and ruin and was destroyed because of his rebellion. Lucifer's nature changed. He became the father of liars and of murderers; a thief, a robber and a killer; deceitful, cruel, fierce and cunning.

The demons were a pre-Adamic race that lived on the earth. God had created them as spirits with bodies. The demons became disembodied spirits. They like to live in a body and may possess unbelievers and oppress believers. God never created an evil spirit. The demons became evil, disembodied spirits by their own choice. They were part of the nations laid low by Lucifer.

When Lucifer rebelled against God, he lost dominion over the earth. God's masterpieces, Adam and Eve, had perfect dominion over all the earth, but a jealous adversary, Lucifer, tricked them into disobeying God. At that point, Lucifer regained the dominion and authority he previously had on earth.

Everybody will be tempted here on earth, and Jesus was no exception. As a young man, Jesus was led by the Holy Spirit into the desert, where for forty days He was tempted by the devil.

> The devil led Him up to a high place and showed Him in
> an instant all the kingdoms of the world. And he said to Him,
> "I will give you all their authority and splendor, for it has been
> given to me, and I can give it to anyone I want to. So if you
> worship me, it will all be yours."
>
> Jesus answered, "It is written: Worship the Lord your God
> and serve Him only" (Luke 4:5–8 NIV).

The devil could talk like that, because Adam had lost all authority to Satan in the Garden of Eden more than four thousand years earlier. That situation changed drastically at the death and the resurrection of Jesus Christ. This is what Jesus said after the resurrection, "All authority in heaven and on earth has been given to me" (Matthew 28:18 NIV). That same authority is given by Jesus Christ to every believer.

Satan is waging a reign of terror upon the inhabitants of the earth. This will greatly intensify in the last days, especially during the Tribulation period. Nevertheless, he is doomed to defeat.

> And I saw an angel coming down out of heaven, having the
> key to the Abyss and holding in his hand a great chain. He
> seized the dragon, that ancient serpent, who is the devil, or
> Satan, and bound him for a thousand years. He threw him
> into the Abyss, and locked and sealed it over him, to keep him
> from deceiving the nations anymore until the thousand years
> were ended. After that, he must be set free for a short time
> (Revelation 20:1–3 NIV).

> When the thousand years are over, Satan will be released from
> his prison and will go out to deceive the nations in the four
> corners of the earth—Gog and Magog—to gather them for
> battle. In numbers they are like the sand on the seashore. They
> marched across the breadth of the earth and surrounded the
> camp of God's people, the city he loves. But fire came down
> from heaven and devoured them. And the devil, who deceived
> them, was thrown into the lake of burning sulfur, where the
> beast and the false prophet had been thrown. They will be
> tormented day and night forever and ever (Revelation 20:7–10
> NIV).

What is the final outcome of Adam and Eve's offspring? The next paragraph shows us specifically the damage done to God's greatest creation: the human beings.

Characteristics of the Fallen Spirit, Mind and Body

1) They no longer display the image and likeness of God. That image and likeness is tarnished and destroyed. "And just as we have borne the likeness of the earthly man [fallen Adam], so shall we bear the likeness of the man from heaven [the last Adam, Jesus Christ]" (1 Corinthians 15:49 NIV).

2) The spirit is still made out of the very essence of God; the mind and body of Adam's offspring are born of corrupt flesh. "Flesh gives birth to flesh, but the Spirit gives birth to spirit" (John 3:6 NIV).

3) The spirit is no longer born of God, but born of flesh. God's life is no longer in him or her. The dwelling place of God is destroyed. The mind and body are subject to sickness and disease.

4) The spirit is dead, eternally. The mind and body age, and death is the final outcome. In the Garden of Eden, God prevented Adam and Eve from eating from the tree of life lest they would never die. Their life span was set at about one thousand years. That life span was further reduced to about one hundred and twenty years at the time of Noah's flood, because of the wickedness and iniquity of the people in those days. "Then the Lord said, 'My Spirit will not contend with man forever, for he is mortal, his days will be a hundred and twenty years'"(Genesis 6:3 NIV).

5) The free will of the spirit and the mind is greatly hampered by evil influences. The body often dictates the course of action that a person takes. The conscience is defiled and polluted. The will is obscured and weak. "They are darkened in their understanding and separated from the life of God because of the ignorance that is in them due to the hardening of their hearts" (Ephesians 4:18 NIV).

6) The spirit, mind and body have lost dominion and authority over the earth and the creatures of the earth. Satan regained that authority. "And he said to him, 'I will give you all their authority

and splendor, for it has been given to me, and I can give it to anyone I want to'" (Luke 4:6 NIV).

7) The spirit, along with mind and body, is held captive by time and space. Acts gives us a good example of when the captivity of time and space is suspended for the mind and body.

8) When they came up out of the water, the Spirit of the Lord suddenly took Philip away, and the eunuch did not see him again, but went on his way rejoicing. Philip, however, appeared at Azotus and traveled about, preaching the gospel in all the towns until he reached Caesarea (Acts 8:39–40 NIV).

9) The spirit, mind and body no longer operate in faith, but in fear. The triune human being is divided. "He answered, 'I heard you in the garden, and I was afraid because I was naked; so I hid'" (Genesis 3:10 NIV).

10) They walk in the flesh. The loving relationship and fellowship with God no longer exist.

11) They are cursed in everything. They are cursed in their spirits, minds and bodies. They are cursed in what they do, their work, their relationships, their finances and their surroundings. Natural disasters are part of the original curse. It is not God's doing, nevertheless many people blame God for it.

> To the woman he said, "I will greatly increase your pain in childbearing; with pain you will give birth to children. Your desire will be for your husband, and he will rule over you."
> To Adam he said, "Because you listened to your wife and ate from the tree about which I commanded you, 'You must not eat from it,'
> Cursed is the ground because of you; through painful toil you will eat of it all the days of your life. It will produce thorns and thistles for you, and you will eat the plants of the field. By the sweat of your brow you will eat your food until you return to the ground" (Genesis 3:16–19 NIV).

The fall of man embodies a curse and a promise. "The seed of the woman" (Genesis 3:15 NIV) will redeem fallen man from the curse.

But it was not until about four thousand years later that the Son of God, Jesus Christ, came to redeem mankind. God needed a structure, an evolved civilization, a people to implement His plan of salvation. God was ready any time, but not His people. Even when He came, many did not receive Him. "He was in the world, and though the world was made through him, the world did not recognize him. He came to that which was his own, but his own did not receive him (John 1:10–11 NIV). But for all who receive and accept Him and still do, restoration is at hand.

The Restoration of Humankind

At the most tragic time in history for humankind, the fall of Adam and Eve, God had a plan to save all humankind. He made the promise, which came to pass about four thousand years later, with the first coming of Jesus Christ, His Son.

God came to humankind's rescue, as He had promised Adam. God cannot, as such, redeem humankind. There had to be a perfect man who could take Adam's place. Around the year A.D. 1, God the Father sent His Son Jesus to earth. God became like you and me. He was stripped of all godly attributes while on earth. Since He was not an offspring of Adam, He was spiritually alive and became the perfect ransom for all humankind. "And he is the head of the body, the church; he is the beginning and the firstborn from among the dead, so that in everything he might have supremacy" (Colossians 1:18 NIV).

"For what the law was powerless to do in that it was weakened by the sinful nature, God did by sending his own Son in the likeness of sinful man to be a sin offering" (Romans 8:3 NIV).

> Who being in very nature God, did not consider equality with God something to be grasped, but made himself nothing, taking the very nature of a servant, being made in human likeness. And being found in appearance as a man, he humbled himself and became obedient to death—even death on a cross! (Philippians 2:6–8 NIV).

In the year A.D. 33, Jesus gave His life for you and me so that we may live. He died by crucifixion. "God made Him who had no sin to be sin for us, so that in him we might become the righteousness of God" (2 Corinthians 5:21 NIV). All hell rejoiced. You see, the devil is not omniscient. He thought that was the end of the Son of God. The devil and the demons' triumph was very short lived. On the third day, Jesus rose from death by the power of the Holy Spirit. "And if the Spirit of him who raised Jesus from the dead is living in you, he who raised Christ from the dead will also give life to your mortal bodies through his Spirit, who lives in you" (Romans 8:11 NIV).

By His blood, death and resurrection, Jesus Christ restored humankind. Darkness changed to light, death to life, hate to love, chains to freedom and despair to joy. He redeemed us from the curse of eternal death, from sickness and disease, and from poverty and bondage. We have the privilege to become sons and daughters of God the Father and brothers and sisters of Jesus Christ. As such we are joint heirs with Jesus Christ.

So why choose Christianity in the first place? Because there is no other faith or religion that can give any human being life of the spirit, mind and body and make us immortal and eternal according to God. "...that everyone who believes in him may have eternal life" (John 3:15 NIV).

"I give them eternal life, and they shall never perish; no one can snatch them out of my hand" (John 10:28 NIV). "For the wages of sin is death, but the gift of God is eternal life in Christ Jesus our Lord" (Romans 6:23 NIV).

"And this is the testimony: God has given us eternal life, and this life is in his Son. He who has the Son has life; he who does not have the Son of God does not have life" (1 John 5:11–12 NIV).

There is no other faith or religion that can give birth to any human being to become a child, a son or a daughter, of God Almighty. "How great is the love the Father has lavished on us, that we should be called children of God! And that is what we are!" (1 John 3:1–2 NIV).

"I will be a Father to you, and you will be my sons and daughters, says the Lord Almighty" (2 Corinthians 6:18 NIV).

There is no other faith or religion that makes any human being a brother and a joint heir with Jesus Christ. "Now if we are children, then we are heirs—heirs of God and co-heirs with Christ, if indeed we share in his sufferings in order that we may also share in his glory" (Romans 8:17 NIV).

There is no other faith or religion that can give any human being spiritual power. Spiritual power is released in our lives, able to transform us and those around us.

- The power of God's forgiveness that sets us free.
- The power that enables us to forgive those who have hurt us.
- The power to resist what we know is wrong.
- The power of God's love, which fills us with love for Him and for others.

- The power of God's Spirit, which brings us the new life of Jesus.
- The power to get wealth to be able to help others and to implement the kingdom of God here on earth. "His divine power has given us everything we need for life" (2 Peter1:3 NIV). There is absolutely no substitute for Christianity.

Self-esteem and Identity

There are people who retain high self-esteem even under extreme conditions of adversity and disadvantage, such as physical disability or extreme poverty. Equally there are many people who seem to have everything in terms of talent, friendships and possessions but who are self-deprecating and even prone to suicidal ideation. The answer in order to understand self-esteem variability and change may be found in the way life events influence higher-order constructs and self-schematics such as low-worthiness, self-determination, and social acceptance. The self-accepting person is fully aware of his or her strengths and weaknesses but still has a high personal regard. The higher-order construct coming from one's spirit that is alive and well is a major construct which most of the time makes the difference.

Every living person is a miracle in the sense that every person overcame many obstacles even before conception. Both the spermatozoa (male cell) and the female egg (female cell) were at the right time at the right place. Only one spermatozoa out of many hundred millions made it and fertilized the egg. In this way billions of people, including you and I, came into being. There is no doubt we are winners right from conception.

Every human being is not only a winner but is also made in the image and likeness of God. Even though that likeness and image was tarnished and partially destroyed by the fall of Adam and Eve it can be restored through the born of God experience.

The born of God believer is a child of God, a son or daughter of God and a brother or sister of Jesus Christ. "How great is the love the Father has lavished on us, that we should be called children of God!" (1 John 3:1 NIV).

We, the sons and daughters of God, are heirs of the promises of God by keeping God's covenant. "You are no longer a slave, but a son; and since you are a son, God has made you also an heir."(Galatians 4:7 NIV).

God the Father did not hesitate to send His Son Jesus Christ to die on the cross to save you: spirit, mind and body.

We are partakers of the divine nature of God. "Through these he has given us his very great and precious promises, so that through them you may participate in the divine nature and escape the corruption in the world caused by evil desires." (2 Peter 1:4 NIV).

Jesus identifies Himself with the least among humans; the aids-afflicted, the leper, the poor, the drug addict, the drunk, the prostitute, the sick and dying, the homeless, the prisoner- they all are a target for 'whatever'. "They also will answer, 'Lord, when did we see you hungry or thirsty or a stranger or needing clothes or sick or in prison, and did not help you?' He will reply, 'I tell you the truth, whatever you did not do for one of the least of these, you did not do for me.' " (Matthew 25:44- 45 NIV).

You are a temple of the Holy Spirit.

"Or do you not know that your body is a temple of the Holy Spirit who is in you whom you have received from God and you are not your own; you were bought at a price. Therefore honor God with your body."(1 Corinthians 6:19 NIV).

God will never forget you nor your needs. "Can a mother forget the baby at her breast and have no compassion on the child she has borne? Though she may forget, I will not forget you." (Isaiah 49:15 NIV).

You may not like yourself nor accept yourself the way you are but God says in His Word that we are made holy. "And by that will we have been made holy through the sacrifice of the body of Jesus Christ once for all." (Hebrews 10:10 NIV).

We have been made perfect. "..because by one sacrifice he has made perfect forever those who are made holy." (Hebrews 10:14 NIV).

God does not remember the breaking of natural and spiritual laws (sins). "Their sins and lawless acts I will remember no more."(Hebrews 10:18 NIV).

God has a plan for each and everyone of us. "For I know the plans I have for you," declares the Lord," plans to proper you and not to harm you, plans to give you hope and a future." (Jeremiah 29:11 NIV).

We are more than conquerors. "No, in all these things [troubles and hardship] we are more than conquerors through him who loved us." (Romans 8:37 NIV).

Many people are apprehensive of the future and are dreadful about dying one day. God promised us an eternal inheritance. "For this reason Christ is the mediator of a new covenant, that those who are called may receive the promised eternal inheritance-now that he has died as a ransom to set them free from the sins committed under the first covenant." (Hebrews

9:15 NIV). Read 'Revelation' in the Bible and ask the Holy Spirit to help you to understand. Revelation tells in detail what the future holds for us.

Positive self-esteem and identity development occur in an individual when an influence ceases to be a control and begins to become a resource for that individual. Religion is a control and not a resource. Many denominations have made a religion out of Christianity and have placed, and still place, their members in bondage. God never forces Himself upon a person nor does He go against anybody's will. Only through a loving personal relationship with the one and only God in three persons: God the Father, God the Son, Jesus Christ, and God the Holy Spirit can and will every human person achieve their real identity with the highest possible self-esteem.

In God's eye every human being is highly valued and precious and nothing can separate the human race as a whole, and in particular every member, from God's unfailing love. "For I am convinced that neither death nor life, neither angels nor the future, nor any powers, neither height nor depth, nor anything else in all creation, will be able to separate us from the love of God that is in Christ Jesus our Lord." (Romans 8:38-39 NIV).

What Are We Taught of Who We Are?

Satan constantly undermines the identity of the believer. He is active to make the believers think that they are sinners, he reminds them of their sins and failures. He is the accuser of the brethren. Many preachers, deceived themselves, deceive their congregation. They quote the Scriptures to give weight to their preaching. "Your righteousness is a filthy rag." According to them it is what verse 64:6 in Isaiah says. This is what that verse really says, "..and all our righteous acts are like filthy rags." It is totally different. It is talking about the sinners (the unbelievers) righteous acts not the believers' acts. Jesus said, "Without Me you can do nothing," As a believer all our righteous acts do have value because we are connected to Jesus. Those preachers also quote Paul but they forget that Paul found the solution in Jesus. Most ill taught believers wind up believing a lie. What you believe in your heart is what you become. It becomes a faith problem. You wind up having no power, a high maintenance believer, a lame duck believer at best. If you believe that you are a sinner, you will keep on sinning. Your relationship with God the Father, God the Son and God the Holy Spirit suffers greatly. You shy away from them.

129

The Catholic Church's scandal of the pedophile priests are victims of their own deception. They are taught that they are sinners. You must go to confession at least a few times per year under sin obligation. As a former Catholic monk I had to go to confession at least ones per week. It was the hardest for me during all my monk years. They expect you to sin. If you tell them that you are sinless, they tell you that you are a liar, you are too proud of yourself. At times I invented sins. Afterwards I could confess that I lied. What a charade! The identity problem exists across all denominations. Martin Luther exhorted his followers to sin and sin vigorously, otherwise they could not be saved. After a while you become totally sin conscious, your focus is totally centered on sin.

The word 'Christian' has become a pejorative to the extension that some Christians do not want to admit in public that they are indeed Christians. The first meaning that comes to mind is sin or hypocrisy. Some businessmen will not hire a Christian because of past negative experiences. It is urgent time for Christians to live up to their true identity and proudly proclaim who they really are. Actions speak louder than any sermon. "In the same way, let your light shine before men, that they may see your good deeds and praise your Father in heaven."(Matthew 5:16 NIV).

We have to take our eyes off sin to focus on Jesus, becoming God conscious. Most Churches are hot houses of sin culture instead of hot houses of righteousness and holiness. Sin scandals in the Churches could be easily eliminated. Dwelling on the problem (sin) will never solve the problem but dwelling on the solution: Jesus, will be easy. "For my yoke is easy and my burden is light."(Matthew 11:30 NIV). It is easier to live a holy and perfect live than to live a sinfulllll live. Most Christians remember the cross but have forgotten the resurrection.

> The day we accepted Jesus we became a new creation: spirit, mind and body. In him you have been circumcised, with a circumcision performed, not by human hand, but **by the complete stripping of your natural self. This is circumcision according to Christ.** You have been buried with him by your baptism; by which, too, you have been raised up with him through your belief in the power of God who raised him from the dead (Colossians 2:11-12 NJB).

We were totally stripped of the natural self: the sin nature. A transubstantiation took place. As the bread and the wine during consecration cease to be bread and wine and become the body and blood of Jesus so are we recreated in the image and likeness of God. On the outside we may not see a difference but in the spirit realm there is a difference of life and death. "and to put on the new self, created to be like God in true righteousness and holiness." (Ephesians 5:24 NIV). The critics are quick to point to Paul and his struggle with sin but they forget that Paul (according to him) lived a holy life. He found the solution: Jesus.

At the resurrection righteousness and holiness was restored in the relationships between God and humanity, between men and women including in their sexual orientation and between people in general.

Jesus: The Solution

Jesus warned us that without Him we can do nothing. "Apart from me you can do nothing." (John 15:5 NIV). We are the branches, He is the vine. The vine does not bear fruit but the branches do. Branches, separated from the vine, wither and become totally useless. We must remain in Him and He will remain in us. Jesus appointed us to go and bear fruit, fruit that will last. (John 15:16 NIV).

How do we remain in Him?

#1
We remain in Him by obeying His commands especially His command of love.

"If you obey my commands, you will remain in my love, just as I have obeyed my Father's commands and remain in his love." (John 15:10 NIV). "My command is this: Love each other as I have loved you." (John 15:12 NIV).

#2
We have to be partakers of His divine nature. "Through these he has given us his very great and precious promises, so that through them you may participate in the divine nature and escape the corruption in the world caused by evil desires." (2 Peter 1:4 NIV). One of those promises is the Eucharist. "Whoever eats my flesh and drinks my blood remains in me, and I in him. Just as the living Father sent me and I live because of the Father, so the one who feeds on me will live because of me." (John 6:56-57 NIV).

The Grace Channel of the Eucharist

The Catholic Church believes that in the Holy Eucharist the body, blood, spirit and divinity of Christ, the God-Man, are truly and substantially present under the appearances of bread and wine. This presence of the entire Christ is by reason of the transubstantiation of the bread and wine into the body and blood of Christ, which is accomplished in the unbloody sacrifice of the Mass. Jesus Himself instituted the Eucharist and requested its repetition (Luke 22:19–20).

The grace channel of the Eucharist is a true sacrifice, a representation of the sacrifice of Christ on the cross, for the ritual elements of the sacrifice are identical with the body and blood of Christ (Hebrews 9:12,14).

The Eucharist is a grace channel of unity. It is meant to unite the faithful more closely each day with God and with one another.

When a priest pronounces the words of Eucharistic consecration, the underlying reality of bread and wine is changed into the body and blood of Christ, given to us in sacrifice. That change has been given the name of 'transubstantiation'. This means that Christ Himself, true God and true Man, is really and substantially present, in a mysterious way, under the appearances of bread and wine.

The sacrifice of the Mass is not merely a ritual that commemorates a past sacrifice. In it, through the ministry of priests, Christ perpetuates the sacrifice of the cross in an unbloody manner. At the same time, the Eucharist is a meal that recalls the Last Supper, celebrates our unity together in Christ and anticipates the messianic banquet of the kingdom. In the Eucharist, Jesus nourishes Christians with His own self, the Bread of Life, so that they may become a people more acceptable to God and filled with greater love of God and others.

> Jesus said to them, "I tell you the truth, unless you eat the flesh of the Son of Man and drink his blood, you have no life in you. Whoever eats my flesh and drinks my blood has eternal life, and I will raise him up at the last day. For my flesh is real food and my blood is real drink. Whoever eats my flesh and drinks my blood remains in me, and I in him" (John 6:53–56 NIV).

Most Protestant denominations do not celebrate the Eucharist as mass. They took, however, one of the main three parts from it, so that their services are centered around that part: the Liturgy of the Word. From the Liturgy of the Eucharist, they retained the money offering, the tithe.

Luther's theory called consubstantiation, the existence of God's presence in the Eucharist, was that the body and blood of Jesus Christ coexisted with the substances of bread and wine. Again, it is in strong contrast to the Catholic view of transubstantiation, that the sacramental bread and wine change into the body and blood of Jesus Christ when consecrated during the mass. Many Protestants, while taking communion, declare that they take the symbols of His body and blood: bread and wine. Jesus' words, in Matthew 26:26–28, clear the controversy.

> While they were eating, Jesus took bread, gave thanks and broke it, and gave it to his disciples, saying, "Take and eat; this is my body." Then he took the cup, gave thanks and offered it to them, saying, "Drink from it, all of you. This is my blood of the covenant, which is poured out for many for the forgiveness of sins." (NIV).

Jesus did not say, "This is the symbol of my body" nor "the symbol of my blood," but "this is my body … this is my blood." It is the spiritual, which is unseen, manifested in the natural, material, which is seen. "Therefore, whoever eats the bread or drinks the cup of the Lord in an unworthy manner will be guilty of sinning against the body and blood of the Lord. For anyone who eats and drinks without recognizing the body of the Lord eats and drinks judgment on himself." (1 Corinthians 11:27,29 NIV). 'Unworthy manner' does not point to the believer being unworthy of receiving the Eucharist but it points to the way the believer receives the Eucharist. The believer is always worthy to receive the Eucharist. Another word for unworthy is inappropriate manner. Unfortunately there are denominations where the minister does not consecrate the bread and the wine. Furthermore they proclaim that they only take part in the symbols of Jesus' flesh and blood making it inappropriate or unworthy for the participants. Some say, "We take the symbols by faith." It means they do not recognize the body and the blood of the Lord. People eat bread and drink wine by faith for breakfast but they do not have communion. If you are part of a denomination where the bread and wine is not consecrated, consecrate it yourself. We are a royal priesthood. "But you are a chosen people, a royal priesthood, a holy nation, a people belonging to God, that you may declare the praises of him who called you out of darkness into his marvelous light." (1 Peter 2:9 NIV). Do it like Jesus told us to do it. **Jesus took bread, gave thanks, broke it and said, "Take this and eat it this is My body which will be given up for you. Do this in**

remembrance of Me." In the same way He took the cup, gave thanks and said, "Take this and drink it. This is My blood, the blood of the sweat in the Garden of Gethsemane, the blood of the crown of thorns, the blood of My back, the blood of My feet, the blood of My hands and the blood of My heart: the blood of the New and Everlasting Covenant which will be shed for you. Do this in remembrance of Me.

The blood of the sweat in the Garden of Gethsemane

"And being in anguish, he prayed more earnestly, and his sweat was like drops of blood falling to the ground." (Luke 22:44 NIV). People sweat blood only when they are subjected to tremendous anguish. One may even die.

The blood of the crown of thorns

The Eucharist is the grace channel of love, the love Jesus Christ has for all humanity. It is represented by His Sacred Heart. The worship and reparation to Christ for men's ingratitude, manifested particularly by indifference to the Holy Eucharist, is directed to the person of Jesus Christ Himself. "..and then twisted together a crown of thorns and set it on his head."(Matthew 27:29 NIV).

The blood of My back

There are thirty nine major diseases. Thirty nine was the number of flogging. Jesus took all diseases upon Himself. "Then he released Barabbas to them. But he had Jesus flogged, and handed him over to be crucified." (Matthew 27:26 NIV).

The blood of My feet

Nailed to the cross in a figurative way, you find yourself immobile, shelved. Moses was shelved for forty years. Remember Jesus achieved the most while hanging on the cross. Your life may be insignificant in the eyes of the world but remember Jesus. Your life may be the most fruitful in the eyes of your Heavenly Father. To be where you ought to be is where you are the most effective for the Kingdom of God. "Here they crucified him, and with him two others- one on each side and Jesus in the middle." (John 19:18 NIV).

The blood of My hands

We work with our hands. Jesus redeemed the work of our hands which enables us to do good. (John 19:18 NIV).

The blood of My heart

Jesus did not die from all the torture He had to endure. He died from a broken heart. Normally the Roman soldiers would break the legs of the crucified person so that that person would die quickly. Once the legs were broken that person would suffocate for not being able to stem himself up for breathing. Jesus was already dead when they came to break his legs. They pierced His side to make sure that He was dead. Jesus died from a broken heart because of all those who reject His love. As a believer you did not contribute to the breaking of His heart but you contribute in consoling Him. "Instead, one of the soldiers pierced Jesus' side with a spear, bringing a sudden flow of blood and water." (John 19:34 NIV). When a believer pronounces the words of consecration God subjects Himself to those words. The greatest miracle takes effect. Think for a moment about the authority and power you have as a believer.

Jesus promised us that he who comes to Him will never hunger nor thirst again. To eat His body and drink His blood must be daily like the manna in the desert. Men do not live by bread alone (natural bread) but by every word (your spiritual nourishment) that proceeds from the mouth of God. There is absolutely no substitute for the body and blood of Jesus even though many may think so and act accordingly. Only the Eucharist gives you life, nothing else not even the Word of God. The Word of God nourishes the life that comes from the Eucharist (Jesus).

#3

We are a temple of the Holy Spirit. "Do you not know that your body is a temple of the Holy Spirit, who is in you, whom you have received from God?" (1 Corinthians 6:19 NIV). " We are the ones who have tasted the heavenly gift, who have shared in the Holy Spirit."(Hebrews 6:4 NIV).

There are times the Holy Spirit acts upon you as a dove, wind, fire or light. For that to happen you must be in a receptive state, in a state where you actively welcome the Holy Spirit. He respects you so much He never forces Himself upon you. He is a real gentleman. Your spirit cannot grow nor mature unless the Holy Spirit is involved with you. He gives you life and freedom, transforms, renews, helps, leads, points out, confirms, shows, teaches, instructs, counsels, enlightens, makes to understand, reveals, gives dreams and visions, intercedes, searches, encourages, strengthens, predicts, warns, keeps you from, admonishes, compels, convicts, witnesses, testifies, determines, brings to remembrance, controls, distributes, cleanses with water, cleanses with fire, sanctifies and gives rest.

The Indwelling

One of the most unusual concept in the Scriptures is the notion of indwelling. That indwelling can be good or evil but no indwelling occurs unless that person welcomes the host. Indwelling is only possible because of our spiritual nature. Not only can a spirit dwell in us human beings we also can dwell by our spirit in another spirit being. "On that day you will realize that I am in my Father, and you are in me, and I am in you." (John 14:20 NIV). That indwelling of God the Father, God the Son and God the Holy Spirit is so complete that we have only one God but three persons. They are one in love, one in attributes but distinct in character. "Holy Father, protect them by the power of your name- the name you gave me- so that they may be one as we are one." (John 17:11 NIV). "That all of them may be one, Father, just as you are in me and I am in you. May they also be in us so that the world may believe that you have sent me. I have given them the glory that you gave me, that they may be one as we are one. I in them and you in me. May they be brought to complete unity to let the world know that you sent me and have loved them even as you have loved me. Father, I want those you have given me to be with me where I am, and to see my glory, the glory you have given me because you loved me before the creation of the world. Righteous Father, though the world does not know you, I know you, and they know that you sent me. I have made you known to them, and will continue to make you known in order that the love you have for me may be in them and that I myself may be in them." (John 17:21-26 NIV).

The Holy Spirit lives in the believers.

"If you love me, you will obey what I command. And I will ask the Father, and he will give you another Counselor to be with you forever- the Spirit of truth. The world cannot accept him, because it neither sees him nor knows him. But you know him, for he lives with you and will be in you." (John 14:15-17 NIV). "Do you not know that your body is a temple of the Holy Spirit, who is in you, whom you have received from God? "(1 Corinthians

6:19 NIV). "And in him you too are being built together to become a dwelling in which God lives by his Spirit." (Ephesians 2:22 NIV). "We know that we live in him [God] and he in us, because he has given us of his Spirit. And we have seen and testify that the Father has sent his Son to be the Savior of the world. If anyone acknowledges that Jesus is the Son of God, God lives in him and he in God." (1 John 4:13-15 NIV).

Where the Holy Spirit dwells there dwell Jesus and the Father also.

"Those who obey his commands live in him [Jesus], and he in them. And this is how we know that he lives in us: We know it by the Spirit he gave us." (1 John 3:24 NIV).

The Father is revealed in Jesus.

"Jesus answered: "Don't you know me, Philip, even after I have been among you such a long time? Anyone who has seen me has seen the Father. How can you say, 'Show us the Father'? Don't you believe that I am in the Father, and that the Father is in me? The words I say to you are not just my own. Rather, it is the Father, living in me, who is doing his work. Believe me when I say that I am in the Father and the Father is in me; or at least believe on the evidence of the miracles themselves." (John 14:9-11 NIV).

"Then Jesus cried out, "When a man believes in me, he does not believe in me only, but in the one who sent me. When he looks at me, he sees the one who sent me." (John 12:44-45 NIV).

"Jesus replied, "If anyone loves me, he will obey my teaching. My Father will love him, and we will come to him and make our home with him." (John 14:23 NIV). Meditate on the indwelling verses frequently and ask the Holy Spirit to give you great understanding concerning this. Make your home with the Holy Spirit, Jesus and the Father.

The indwelling is a unique characteristic of the Christian faith. No other faith can claim this uniqueness. There are no other gods. All what religions can claim may be a demonic or satanic indwelling which will lead to deception and destruction. "As soon as Judas took the bread, Satan entered into him" (John 13:27 NIV). "When an evil spirit comes out of a man, it goes through arid places seeking rest and does not find it. Then it says, 'I will return to the house I left. When it arrives, it finds the house swept clean and put in order. Then it goes and takes seven other spirits more wicked than itself, and they go in and live there. And the final condition of that man is worse than the first." (Luke 11:24-26 NIV). When God dwells in a person no evil spirit can dwell in that person. We are so privileged to be created by a loving God and to be His sons and daughters.

Be Holy Because I Am Holy

For most Christians the command from God, "Be holy because I am holy" (1Peter 1:15 NIV) is not even considered. I have never heard any preacher, teacher, apostle or evangelist exalt the people to be holy. What I heard over and over again was how great sinners we Christians are, worthless and good for nothing. To make their point they all quoted Paul the Apostle, "I do not understand what I do. For what I want to do I do not do, but what I hate I do. I know that nothing good lives in me, that is in my sinful nature. What a wretched man I am!" (Romans 7:15,18,24 NIV). Satan, the devil, the great deceiver is working overtime through deceived teachers. "For the time will come when men will not put up with sound doctrine. Instead, to suit their own desires, they will gather around them a great number of teachers to say what their itching ears want to hear. They will turn their ears away from the truth and turn aside to myths."(2 Timothy 4:3-4 NIV).

Who are we the born of God believers in reality? Are we still the sinners we are told we are? The born of God birth does not only involve our spirit but our mind and our body as well. It is not an adoption like in the natural where a couple adopts a child. That couple is not and will never be the biological parents of that child. For the born of God believer God the Father becomes the spiritual as well as the new biological Father. A transubstantiation takes place at the moment of birth, similar to the transubstantiation that takes place when bread and wine are consecrated. They become the body and blood of Jesus Christ and are no longer bread and wine even though they retain the outer appearance of bread and wine. When a surgeon cuts into the flesh of a believer that flesh is different from the flesh of an unbeliever. I have a friend who is an undertaker. He told me that he can tell from the odor the cadavers emanate who is a Christian and who is not. We Christians are no longer a sin-species but a Christ-species, a God-species. Most Bible sin verses no longer apply to us. We are not sinners anymore but Christ-like people, righteous people. "For just as through the disobedience of the one man the many were made sinners, so also through the obedience of the one man the many will be made righteous." (Romans 5:9 NIV). "You were taught, with regard to your former way of life, to put off your old self, which is being corrupted by its deceitful desires; to be made new in the attitude of your minds; and to put on the new self, created to be like God in true righteousness and holiness."(Ephesians 4:22-24 NIV). We have to change the attitude of our minds and focus on righteousness and holiness and not on sinfulness. If we sin that still does not make us sinners in the same way if we bark that does not make us dogs either. We can start by changing the 'sinner's prayer' to 'life-giving prayer'. After Paul made his disconcerting statement in Romans 7:15,18 and 24 he also gave us the solution to that problem we all face. It is verse 25, "Thanks be to God-through Jesus Christ our Lord!" (NIV). Here is another quote from the Apostle Paul, a quote every preacher should be familiar with and preach to their congregation. "Our conscience testifies that we have conducted ourselves in the world, and especially in our relations with you, in the holiness and sincerity that are from God." (2 Corinthians 1:12 NIV). Paul emphasizes holiness as a key factor in his relations with other people, a far cry from a sinful mentality. Many Protestants become born of God by saying the Sinner's Prayer but are not baptized at all which makes it extremely difficult for them not to sin anymore. Because one of the effects of baptism is 'the complete stripping of the natural self' which does not occur if a person is not baptized. When a person keeps on sinning that person is not born of God at all. "No one who is born of God will continue to sin."(1 John 3:9 NIV). Radical human sinfulness as taught by Calvinistic doctrine implies that Jesus' sacrifice on the cross and His resurrection are flawed in that it was unable to restore humankind to its proper state: holy and perfect in God's eyes, sons and daughters of God.

Most preachers want us to believe that holiness is not on God's agenda for the believers. Even the meaning of the word 'holy' is hardly understood or not understood at all. Here are some of the meanings of the word 'holy': of divine origin, saintly character, consecrated to God, set apart, awesome, beautiful, whole, perfect and being yourself. At most out of all these meanings 'set apart' is the one most of the preachers agree on. It is also the one which requires the least effort from anyone. In the next verse 'set apart' is quoted separate from holy. "Such a high priest meets our needs_ one who is holy, blameless, pure, set apart from sinners, exalted above the heavens." (Hebrews 7:26 NIV). A believer is of divine origin, consecrated to God, set apart from sinners, and he or she can achieve saintly character with the result of becoming awesome, beautiful, whole and perfect. 'Being yourself' fits into 'whole and perfect'. How can a person be whole and perfect while trying constantly to be someone else. You cannot fulfill God's divine calling by trying to be what or whom you are not. Everybody is special and unique: an original and not a clone. A positive self-esteem and identity must be yours to love yourself as God intended it to be. He gave us the command, "Love your neighbor as yourself."(Matthew 19:19 NIV). How can you love your neighbor as yourself when you hate yourself?

Self-esteem is the judgment people make about their own worth. Self-worth lies in the eye of the beholder. Self-esteem comes from the inside. One makes up a concept, the self-concept. It is what one thinks one is, ones abilities, failures and traits. The real self is the self one really is and the ideal self is the self one would like to be. Self-esteem is seen as an indicator of mental health as it carries properties of emotional adjustment, general coping with life and life's satisfaction and well-being.

Identity is an internal, self-constructed dynamic organization of values, beliefs, drives and traits, unique to that individual. Identity has its roots in identification which is a process by which a person acquires the characteristics of another person or persons. As an individual grows up and matures, he or she switches from identification to identity.

People's identity and self-esteem are composed from a uniquely personal and symbolic interpretation of an influence. No two persons are affected and react in the same way by the same influence. **Positive self-esteem and identity development occur in an individual when an influence ceases to be a control and begins to become a resource for that individual**. A person who perceives himself or herself as having little or no control over an influence will suffer a loss of self-esteem and does not establish a positive identity.

A bi-directional movement of the individual/influence relationship affects identity and self-esteem. A person interacts with the influence and the influence interacts with the individual. As a result identity and self-esteem are being shaped and go through change because of psychological, physical, social, emotional and spiritual interactions.

Everybody should be able to find ways of experiencing positive self-esteem as they progress through life. Societies and cultures set rules, laws and ways of life that do not always allow individuals total freedom to choose a route towards positive self-esteem and identity formation.

Social laws and traditions pressure individuals to conform through their appearance, abilities and behavior. Adherence to any cultural or societal tradition that hinders rather than furthers positive self-esteem and identity is to be avoided. It is preferable to be labeled as an outcast, an eccentric, or an incompetent than regarded a slave to fashion, a victim to coercion, or lacking substance or character.

Men and women can develop, grow and gain self-esteem and identity as individuals throughout life without being stereotyped, labeled, categorized and evaluated on the basis of gender or age. That route will take them not in a straight line but they will experience ups and downs, and lefts and rights, but as long as they forge ahead it will provide them richness of experience, personal growth and self-knowledge.

Self-esteem and identity are a product of the spirit, the mind and the body: the total human being. They start at the mental plane where they are fought and built in conjunction with the physical body and reach the culmination in the spirit realm.

Holiness is at the reach of anyone with the help of the Holy Spirit as the teacher. "..and who through the Spirit of holiness was declared with power to be the Son of God by his resurrection from the dead: Jesus Christ our Lord. (Romans 1:4 NIV). The Holy Spirit is the Spirit of holiness and He can and will be your teacher and helper if only you let Him.

How Do Righteousness, Blamelessness and Holiness Fit Together?

The account of the young rich ruler in Matthew can give us insight. "Now a man came up to Jesus and asked, "Teacher, what must I do to get eternal life?" "Why do you ask me about what is good?" Jesus replied. "There is only One who is good. If you want to enter life, obey the commandments." Which ones?" the man inquired. Jesus replied, "'Do not murder, do not commit adultery, do not steal, do not give false testimony, honor your father and mother,' and 'love your neighbor as yourself.' "All these I have kept," the young man said. "What do I still lack?" Jesus answered, "If you want to be perfect [holy], go, sell your possessions and give to the poor, and you will have treasures in heaven. Then come, and follow me." When the man heard this, he went away sad, because he had great wealth." (Matthew 19:16-22 NIV). When the young man asked, "What good thing must I do to get eternal life." I would expect Jesus to answer, "Believe in me and be baptized." But no, Jesus replied, "No one is good except One meaning God. Jesus brought the focus on God away from things. Preachers use this passage to proof that all people are bad: sinners. Yes they are but only as long as they are not born of God. The young man obeyed the commandments which made him blameless but not perfect [holy].

Unconditional love must come into play for holiness to be achieved. What Jesus required from this young man seems to be harsh. The passage reveals that things had a hold on the young man. Money was not the problem but the love of money was. Jesus wanted him to be free from bondage and at the same time promised a hundred fold in this life in addition to eternal life. "And everyone who has left houses or brothers or sisters or father or mother or children or fields for my sake will receive a hundred times as much and will inherit eternal life. " (Matthew 19:29 NIV).

Righteousness is given as a gift to anyone who becomes born of God. That righteousness is sustained by obedience to the teaching of Jesus Christ. Righteousness leads to holiness and holiness to eternal life. "Blessed are those who hunger and thirst for righteousness for they will be filled." (Matthew 5:6 NIV). The born of God believers are the righteous ones. "Therefore, I urge you brothers, in view of God's mercy, to offer your bodies as living sacrifices, holy and pleasing to God_ this is your spiritual act of worship." (Romans 12:1 NIV). It means to offer the parts of our bodies to Him as instruments of righteousness and not as instruments of wickedness.

In a nutshell: blamelessness = not doing bad things

> righteousness = doing the right things
> holiness = unconditional love in all relationships with God and men and in all what we do which is contained in God's primary command: love your God with all your heart, with all your mind and with all your body and love your neighbor as yourself.

Holiness has to do with our will and our heart (intentions). It does not mean that we never fail, never forget, never make mistakes, never show emotions, never have thoughts and desires contrary to God's will nor does it mean that we become supermen. It means we hunger and thirst for righteousness and holiness. It means we do everything in our ability to achieve God's perfect will in our lives and in the lives of others and to build His kingdom.

If you struggle to be holy, you have the wrong goal set for yourself. Holiness and righteousness is through grace by faith. It is a gift from God. Many believe it cannot be achieved. They insult the Spirit of Grace. "..and who has insulted the Spirit of Grace." (Hebrews 10:29 NIV). Holiness and righteousness are a by-product of your relationship with God the Father, God the Son and God the Holy Spirit. The Ten Commandments become a promise rather than a law. Remember that you can do anything through Him who gives you strength. "I can do everything through him who gives me strength." (Philippians 4:13 NIV).

Know God

What does it mean to know God? What does it mean to know Jesus? The word 'to know' has many meanings.

#1 For a Christian to know Jesus means to be born again. But that is not all, there   is a lot more to it than that.

#2 "But he had no union with her until she gave birth to a son." (Matthew 1:24 NIV) Some translation say, "he did not know her." In this sense knowing means: having sexual intercourse with your spouse.

#3 It can mean being informed, getting scent or wind of, having the facts about God. Be acquainted with and having knowledge of.

#4 You need no proof, you are certain, you are apodictic. Some people may ask, "Can you prove God? You need no proof because you know God.

#5 You understand, you comprehend, you conceive.

#6 Be close friend, be inseparable.

#7 Identify with Jesus. You are of the same Christ species.

#8 Experience Jesus, the Father and the Holy Spirit with your five natural and spiritual senses.

Scriptures give us the facts about God the Father, God the Son and God the Holy Spirit. It reveals the teaching, the character and the temperament of Jesus. It portraits Jesus as the Son of Man. Not only learn we about His frustration with the slow learning of the disciples, His outburst of anger in the house of the Father, His love and compassion for the sinners, the oppressed, the sick, the blind, the disabled, the marginalized. He has room in His heart for everybody. We hear the slogan: it's all about Jesus, no it's all about us and Jesus, God the Father and God the Holy Spirit.

God is unpredictable. His thoughts are not our thoughts, His ways are not our ways. God's ways violate the human justice because of grace.

Knowing Jesus, the Father and the Holy Spirit is spending time with them, be close to them, talk to them, confide in them, touch them through the suffering humanity, be grieved when they are grieved, delight in good and not in evil.

When you talk to God, be real. Do not put on a show. Some treat God as if He is mental. If you talk to your spouse like some talk to God, your spouse would get you committed to the mental institution. Others, when they pray, put on the monkey anointing: weird expressions and behavior. Leave that to the monkeys.

We are all individuals, not clones. Therefore our relationship with Jesus, the Father and the Holy Spirit are also individualistic and unique. God sees us so beautiful. Jesus showed me a concrete example of how He sees us. He selected an overweight, out of shape, less than average looking woman (on the ugly side) over fifty. In the natural she was ugly. Suddenly that same woman looked so beautiful, extremely beautiful and pretty. It lasted for about a minute. We cannot judge a person in regards to beauty with the natural eyes. Our physical body is the seed for a glorified body. The uglier the 'seed' the more beautiful will be the glorified body. If you are disabled, distorted, plain ugly do not be discouraged. The most beautiful, the most agile, the most pretty glorified body is awaiting you.

For a relationship to be meaningful and rewarding any person must know his or her true identity that he or she is a temple of the Holy Spirit where Jesus and the Father dwell. Enjoy the continual awareness of God's indwelling, this vibrant reality of truth. They also must partake in the divine nature of God Almighty. Not by ideas or doctrine but as the source of life: His sustaining presence of all our lives.

Scriptures do not get you to know God but experience does: relationships cultivated. Take a marriage manual for example. It does not matter how much you study it, unless you transfer it into experience, into cultivated relationship with your spouse it does you no good. The verse in Matthew 7:22-23 (NIV) is a very good illustration. "Many will say to me on that day, 'Lord, Lord, did we not prophesy in your name, and in your name drive out demons and perform many miracles? Then I will tell them plainly, 'I never knew you. Away from me, you evildoers!' They were doing everything according to Scriptures but lacked love. They did not know Jesus. They pursuit the gifts but forgot the Giver.

Enoch walked with God for three hundred years. He did not die. Most biographies end with the words, "then he died." Not so with Enoch. Walk with God and you will get to know Him and surely you will not die.

"Enoch walked with God 300 years and had other sons and daughters. Altogether, Enoch lived 365 years. Enoch walked with God; then he was no more, because God took him away." (Genesis 5:22-24 NIV).

Eternal Purpose

Have you ever wondered why young people die, why excellent Christians get cancer and other fatal diseases, why a mother, a father, a child is suddenly taken from the family by dying unexpectedly? May be the most disconcerting of them all is why did God not heal them all and prevent their demise? I asked many people including preachers, "Why did God not heal so and so?" The answers were numerous: lack of faith, sin in the person's life, unforgiveness and so on. Jesus healed many sinners, while they were sinners. He told them after they were healed, "Sin no more." So sin is definitely not the problem. Many conceded, "We do not know the answer." Many people create their own hindrances by believing wrongly therefore act wrongly too. There are Scriptures verses that tell us the real answers: the truth.

"..according to his eternal purpose which he accomplished in Christ Jesus our Lord." (Ephesians 3:11 NIV).

"Now in him who is able to do immeasurably more than we ask or imagine, according to his power that is at work within us." (Ephesians 3:20 NIV).

"And we know that in all things God works for the good of those who love him, who have been called according to his purpose." (Romans 8:28 NIV).

We have to trust God in everything that He works for the ultimate eternal good in our lives.

"God will work in you to will and to act [without violating your free will] according to his good purpose." (Philippians 2:13 NIV). I must stress that it is not our good purpose but God's good purpose. God has always our ultimate eternal good in mind, not just as an individual but also as a corporate entity: His body with Jesus as the head. We are called according to His purpose, called to live a holy life. "who has saved us and called us to a holy life." (2 Timothy 1:9 NIV).

Your life becomes a grace channel, a sacrament were rivers of living waters gush out from you. At times you may not even be aware of it. God's purpose for your life may be the baptism of blood.

The Baptism of Blood

The Bible mentions three baptisms: the baptism of water, the baptism of the Holy Spirit and the baptism of blood. The baptism of water you receive at the time you are born of God; by your asking, receiving and accepting Jesus Christ (Christ in you, His responsibility) and through the baptism you are baptized into Christ (you in Christ, your responsibility). "You are all sons of God through faith in Christ Jesus, for all of you who were baptized into Christ have clothed yourselves with Christ." (Galatians 3:26–27 NIV). The baptism of the Holy Spirit should be received after that. These two baptisms are right at the start of your Christian life and walk, but the baptism of blood may occur at any time of your life, or it may not occur at all. The baptism of blood is the least known and is often misunderstood or not understood at all.

There are two distinct aspects of the baptism of blood, having to do with the respective recipients. One category is for those who give their lives for Jesus Christ rather than apostatize and deny Him. It is the sacrifice of one's life. Many became martyrs during the persecutions, and many become martyrs today. They may be Christians, or they may be like the thief on the cross and give their lives at the last moment for Christ and be saved through the baptism of blood, martyrdom for Christ.

The other category is for those who live their lives as living testaments of the faith but die of natural causes. They are exclusively Christians. Martyrdom is an exceptional gift and the perfect proof of love. Martyrdom may be applied to those who die at the hands of persecutors or to those who die slowly at the hands of circumstances in the service of Jesus Christ for others. Laying down one's life for Christ and others is the ultimate sacrifice and gift one can make. "For God so loved the world that he gave his one and only Son, that whoever believes in him shall not perish but have eternal life." (John 3:16 NIV).

"Greater love has no one than this, that he lay down his life for his friends" (John 15:13 NIV).

The blood baptism has to do with dying literally and suffering. The human nature is opposed to dying and to suffering, so it is not something very popular or something to look forward to. All death and suffering have their origin in the fall of Adam and Eve. It is a negative, but even from a negative, God can make a positive. Jesus Christ through His passion, death and resurrection brought salvation to the human race, and so through our death and suffering He can bring that salvation to people.

Many Christians entertain the notion that since Christ suffered for us, so we do not have to suffer. In fact, I have never met anyone who did not suffer one way or another. Those people base their understanding on the following verse. "He carried our infirmities and bore our diseases." (Matthew 8:17 NIV paraphrased). This verse does not say that we will have no infirmities or diseases; it simply means that our infirmities and diseases are not in vain like those of the unbelievers. The believers do not suffer in vain.

"And by his wounds we are healed." (Isaiah 53:5 NIV). You cannot be healed unless you are sick in the first place. After being sick we have at our disposition healing purchased for us by Jesus Christ through His wounds.

Why do we suffer?

Originally suffering entered the human race through the fall of Adam and Eve. Suffering is not something God created or God put on people. At best God allows suffering, but He not only allows suffering, He also turns it into something creative, positive and good. We may suffer for many reasons. We may suffer for the gospel.

> "Blessed are you who when people insult you, persecute you and falsely say all kind of evil against you because of me. Rejoice and be glad, because great is your reward in heaven, for in the same way they persecuted the prophets who where before you." (Matthew 5:11–12.NIV).

We suffer because of our shortcomings and faults. Sickness and disease are often brought on by our faulty living habits. We also suffer because of others, which is hard to accept and hard to forgive.

How should a Christian suffer?

Since we all suffer at one time or another, let's look at Jesus—how He suffered. Jesus used suffering, death and His resurrection to bring redemption and salvation to the human race. He looked forward to His passion and death not for suffering's sake but for the glory it would bring to the human race.

"I have come to bring fire on the earth, and how I wish it were already kindled! But I have a baptism to undergo, and how distressed I am until it is completed." (Luke 12:49–50 NIV).

"I have come to bring fire to the earth, and how I wish it were blazing already. There is a baptism I must still receive, and what constraint I am under until it is completed!" (Luke 12:49–50 NJB). Jesus was distressed and under great constraint to see it happen. It was something He had to do, to undergo, He came to earth for it.

When Peter the Apostle tried to prevent Jesus from receiving the baptism of blood, he received the greatest rebuke.

> He then began to teach them that the Son of Man must suffer many things and be rejected by the elders, chief priests and teachers of the law, and that he must be killed and after three days rise again. He spoke plainly about this, and Peter took him aside and began to rebuke him.
>
> But when Jesus turned and looked at his disciples, he rebuked Peter, "Get behind me, Satan!" he said. "You do not have in mind the things of God, but the things of men." (Mark 8:31–33 NIV).

Even though Jesus looked forward to His passion, at the time it really happened, He was troubled to death and asked His Father to take this cup away from Him.

> He took Peter, James and John along with him, and he began to be deeply distressed and troubled. "My soul is overwhelmed with sorrow to the point of death," he said to them. "Stay here and keep watch."
>
> Going a little farther, he fell to the ground and prayed that if possible the hour might pass from him. "Abba, Father," he said, "everything is possible for you. Take this cup from me. Yet not what I will, but what you will." (Mark 14:33–36 NIV).

Some people may say, "That's for Jesus not for us."

> Then James and John, the sons of Zebedee, came to him, "Teacher," they said, "we want you to do for us whatever we ask."
>
> "What do you want me to do for you?" he asked.

They replied, "Let one of us sit at your right and the other at your left in your glory."

"You do not know what you are asking, "Jesus said. "Can you drink the cup I drink or be baptized with the baptism I am baptized with?"

"We can," they answered.

Jesus said to them, "You will drink the cup I drink and be baptized with the baptism I am baptized with, but to sit at my right or left is not for me to grant. These places belong to those for whom they have been prepared." (Mark 10:35–40 NIV.)

James and John, the sons of Zebedee, two of Jesus' disciples were baptized with the baptism Jesus was baptized with, the baptism of blood. There are many disciples of Jesus both then and now who were and are baptized with the baptism of blood. It is a great privilege and honor. Most of those baptized with the baptism of blood are martyrs not by choice but by circumstances. There is, however, a very small group who are baptized by choice. Their love for God is so great, their likeness in the image of God so profound, that they are given by God through grace (divine influence) the stigmata. Stigmata comes from a Greek word meaning marks. It refers to the wounds that appear on the flesh of individuals, either all the wounds or some, visible or invisible, but painful—at different times and seasons more painful. These wounds correspond to the wounds suffered by Jesus Christ at the crucifixion. There are more than 300 well-documented cases worldwide. St. Catherine of Sienna requested from our Lord that the stigmata be invisible, not evident on her body. A most recent person with the stigmata was Padre Pio, an Italian Catholic monk. I personally wrote him a letter, and he responded. He also operated in the gifts of the Holy Spirit and often revealed in the confessional the penitent's hidden shortcomings and sins. Are there any Bible examples of persons who bore the stigmata? Yes, Paul the Apostle. "Finally, let no one cause me trouble, for I bear on my body the marks [stigmata] of Jesus." (Galatians 6:17 NIV). They were not spiritual or invisible wounds but visible because Paul says, "on my body."

Some people think that suffering is controversial but not so according to the Scriptures.

"Dear friends do not be surprised at the painful trial you are suffering, as though something strange were happening to you. But rejoice that you participate in the sufferings of Christ, so that you may be overjoyed when his glory is revealed (1 Peter 4:12–13 NIV).

"So then, those who suffer according to God's will should commit themselves to their faithful Creator and continue to do good." (1 Peter 4:19 NIV).

"Now I rejoice in what was suffered for you, and I fill up in my flesh what is still lacking in regard to Christ's afflictions, for the sake of his body, which is the church." (Colossians 1:24 NIV).

> Now if we are children, then we are heirs—heirs of God and co-heirs with Christ, if indeed we share in his suffering in order that we may also share in his glory. I consider that our present sufferings are not worth comparing with the glory that will be revealed in us." (Romans 8:17–18 NIV).

> "For it has been granted to you on behalf of Christ not only to believe in him, but also to suffer for him, since you are going through the same struggle you saw I had, and now hear that I still have." (Philippians 1:29–30 NIV).

"I want to know Christ and the power of his resurrection and the fellowship of sharing in his suffering, becoming like him in his death, and so, somehow, to attain to the resurrection from the dead." (Philippians 3:10–11 NIV).

"To this you were called, because Christ suffered for you, leaving you an example, that you should follow in his steps." (1Peter 2:21 NIV).

"It is better, if it is God's will, to suffer for doing good than for doing evil." (1Peter 3:17 NIV).

"Therefore, since Christ suffered in his body, arm yourselves also with the same attitude, because he who has suffered in his body is done with sin." (1Peter 4:1 NIV).

These Bible verses clearly indicate how a Christian should conduct himself when faced with suffering:

- "Participate in the suffering of Christ." (1 Peter 4:12-13).
- "According to the will of God." (1 Peter 4:19).
- "To supplement what is lacking to the body of Christ." (Colossians 1:24).
- "Share in Christ's suffering." (Romans 8:17-18).

- "Suffer for him." (Philippians 1:29-30).
- "Fellowship in his suffering." (Philippians 3:10-11).
- "To follow in his footsteps." (1 Peter 2:21).
- "Trust in him, commit yourself to him." (1 Peter 4:19).
- "While you suffer, continue to do good." (1 Peter 4:19).

The disciple is not above the master. We all suffer, but not all are candidates for the baptism of blood. Candidates are sons of God. They become the seed for a great harvest of souls. "I tell you the truth, unless a kernel of wheat falls to the ground and dies, it remains only a single seed. But if it dies, it produces many seeds." (John 12:24 NIV).

Who are sons of God? Those who are led by the Holy Spirit, the peacekeepers and those who love their enemies. "You are all sons of God through faith in Christ Jesus." (Galatians 3:26 NIV).

"..because those who are led by the Spirit of God are sons of God." (Romans 8:14 NIV).

"Blessed are the peacemakers for they will be called sons of God." (Matthew 5:9 NIV).

"...love your enemies and pray for those who persecute you, that you may be sons of your Father in heaven." (Matthew 5:45 NIV).

Only sons of God are priesthood. The primary function of the priests is worship offered up by the Holy Spirit through Jesus Christ to the Father. "For all their (laity's) works, prayers, and apostolic endeavors, their ordinary married and family life, their daily labor, their mental and physical relaxation, if carried out in the Spirit, and even the hardships of life, if patiently borne—all of these become spiritual sacrifices acceptable through Jesus Christ. During the Celebration of the Eucharist, these sacrifices are most lovingly offered to the Father along with the Lord's body. The faithful offer the divine Victim to God and offer themselves along with it." (Broderick, 1987, p. 198).

"You also, like living stones, are being built into a spiritual house to be a holy priesthood, offering spiritual sacrifices acceptable to God through Jesus Christ." (1 Peter 2:5 NIV).

"But you are a chosen people, a royal priesthood, a holy nation, a people belonging to God."(1 Peter 2:9 NIV).

The Eucharist is celebrated on a continual basis because of time zones. So at any time, the sons of God, the royal priesthood, can offer up together with the sacrifice of Jesus Christ everything which makes up their life—the physical, mental and spiritual suffering, all good things and all bad things. You may wonder how exactly; here is how.

Very few people are taught how they should use the mind. We take it for granted that everybody knows how to think properly, and we do not realize that all our thought processes are governed by specific principles common to all human beings. Scriptures declare, "My people perish for lack of knowledge." (Hosea 4:6 paraphrased NIV). Even those who get the knowledge, very few know how to process it properly.

Everything that happens to us, everything that is said to us and everything that we sense with our senses can be regarded as influence having an effect on us. We are constantly bombarded with influence, good and bad. It is clear if we do not know how to process that influence, we are not functioning properly, and a lot of that influence is wasted but not only wasted; it becomes detrimental to us and eventually may even destroy us. We will not live our life to its full potential physically, mentally and spiritually. (reprinted from 'Christianity: Success or Failure' by the same author).

You can become a secret agent for the kingdom of God. Everywhere you go, your private life, your public life, your family, the market place wherever your feet tread. You can change the world, your world from the inside out. The kingdom of God can be seen by your eyes or it can be seen by its effects or even tasted by its flavor. "When Jesus asked, "What is the kingdom of God like? What shall we compare it? It is like a mustard seed, which a man took and planted in his garden. It grew and became a tree, and the birds of the air perched in its branches." Again he asked, "What shall I compare the kingdom of God? It is like yeast that a woman took and mixed into a large amount of flour until it worked all through the dough." (Luke 13:18-21 NIV). "You are the salt of the earth. But if the salt loses its saltiness, how can it be made salty again? It is no longer good for anything, except to be thrown out and trampled by men." (Matthew 5:13 NIV).

- making disciples of all men and women
"Therefore go and make disciples of all nations, baptizing them in the name of the Father and of the Son and of the Holy Spirit." (Matthew 28:19 NIV). You build the kingdom of God by evangelizing all nations so that everybody becomes born of God. Make sure those you made disciples do not park at this stage but continue their walk with God and reach maturity.

-teach them to obey everything Jesus commanded

"..and teaching them to obey everything I have commanded you." (Matthew 28:19 NIV). This is what gets you in the kingdom of God permanently. The Reformation introduced heresy into the body of Christ by teaching all that is needed for making it to heaven is saying the 'Sinners prayer'. Everybody will be judged by his deeds (works) and those works good or bad determine where and how a person spend eternity either in the kingdom of God or in the kingdom of Satan. John Bevere had a vision. He saw millions of born again Christians going to hell for not working out their salvation by building God's kingdom on earth.

The Last Word

God has always the last word. He is in control and He put us humans in charge on the earth. My friend told me that he too has always the last word with his wife: "yes dear." Once you align your will with God's will you enter, you participate in God's eternal purpose. There are absolutely no hindrances on God's side to do greater things than Jesus did. People create their own hindrances by what they believe and not believe. Jesus is the solution for you to do greater things than He did. You must also realize that not everybody has the same assignment, the same gifts. We are a body (the body of Christ, with Jesus as the head) with many different parts and functions. Remember that Jesus was most effective while hanging on the cross, while being nailed to the cross. In His greatest weakness He was the most effective: He saved the world and humanity. So take courage you are precious, important and unique, worthy of His love and kindness. Know Jesus, the Father and the Holy Spirit and you will do greater things than Jesus did. You have the advantage in His name and you operate under the New Covenant.

Resources

The Holy Bible
New International Version ®. NIV ®.
Copyright © 1973, 1978, 1984 by International Bible Society.
Used by permission of Zondervan Publishing House. All rights reserved.
Grand Rapids, Michigan

How To and When
Gustav Shakefoot (2006)
Holy Fire Publishing

Christianity: Success or Failure?
Gustav Shakefoot (2006)
Holy Fire Publishing

Spirit, Mind and Body
Gustav Shakefoot (2007)
Holy Fire Publishing

Who is Your Father?
Gustav Shakefoot (2008)
Holy Fire Publishing

Other Books Available by the Same Author

"Christianity: Success or Failure? "
This is a book for all Christians regardless of their denominational affiliation as well as anyone who wishes to know more about Christianity. I hope it will bring a much needed unity in the divided Body of Christ. At the same time it provides a clear roadmap of how to live, on a personal level, the Christian life: your walk with God. (Available online: astore.amazon. com/christianpubl-20)

"How To and When"
A practical guide to increase your intelligence and especially the intelligence of your children. I have never met a person with a high I.Q. who achieved top ability (intelligence) through other methods and means than the ones outlined in 'How To & When'. It will give any parent the option to make their child a genius. Remember that ability does not happen by chance. If your child is less fortunate and suffers from a brain disorder or brain injury (autism, down syndrome and others) this book is the best of its kind to provide effective therapy.
(Available online: astore.amazon.com/christianpubl-20)

"Spirit, Mind and Body" provides basic knowledge about the human nature. That knowledge is essential in order to lead a victorious and successful life. Part one deals specifically with the spirit, mind and body. Part two looks at puberty: a maturational phase everybody will go through. Part three examines self-esteem and personal identity, and part four shows how to transform any negative traumatic events in a person's life into a positive influence.

'Spirit, Mind and Body' is some sort of a mosaic where each part brings to light a different value, a different color and a different texture thus complementing each other to form a uniquely crafted picture of the human spirit, mind and body.

(Available online: astore.amazon.com/christianpubl-20)

"Who Is Your Father?"

Many of society's ills can be traced back to fatherlessness. Unfortunately we live in a mostly fatherless generation. Fathers are very critical in any person's life. We did not choose our biological father, we can choose our spiritual father but most of all we can and should choose our heavenly Father. If we do not choose God the Father we automatically choose Satan as our father: the father of lies. There are no substitutes for the biological father nor for God the Father. The physical presence of the biological father is required for anyone to mature properly and so is the presence of God the Father required to mature spiritually.

'Who is your Father?' will help you to make that choice.

(Available online: astore.amazon.com/christianpubl-20)

"Love & Sex in Marriage"

Perfect Guide for Love and Sexual Fulfillment in Marriage Relationships between spouses are greatly influenced by a number of components such as: sexuality, male and female physiology, temperaments, psychology, love languages etc.. All carry great potential for total communion: spirit, mind and body.

(Available online: Trafford.com/08-1090)

Author Contact Information

e-mail: gustavgrun@yahoo.ca